BEN SIRA AND DEMOTIC WISDOM

λ

SOCIETY OF BIBLICAL LITERATURE
MONOGRAPH SERIES

James L. Crenshaw, Editor

Number 28
BEN SIRA AND DEMOTIC WISDOM

by
Jack T. Sanders

Jack T. Sanders

BEN SIRA
AND DEMOTIC WISDOM

Scholars Press
Chico, California

BEN SIRA AND DEMOTIC WISDOM

by
Jack T. Sanders

© 1983
The Society of Biblical Literature

Library of Congress Cataloging in Publication Data

Sanders, Jack T.
  Ben Sira and demotic wisdom.

  (Society of Biblical Literature monograph series ; no. 28)
  Includes bibliographical references and index.
  1. Bible.   O.T.   Apocrypha.   Ecclesiasticus—Criticism,
interpretation, etc. 2. Wisdom literature—Relation to Egyptian
literature. I. Title. II. Series.
BS1765.2.S26 1983   229'.406   82-21464
ISBN 0-89130-585-8
ISBN 0-89130-586-6 (pbk.)

Printed in the United States of America

This book is very fondly
and affectionately dedicated to

Collin,

who was the first to know.

CONTENTS

Abbreviations

AcOr	*Acta orientalia*
AnBib	Analecta biblica
ANE	Ancient Near East
ANET	J. B. Pritchard (ed.), *Ancient Near Eastern Texts*
APOT	R. H. Charles (ed.), *Apocrypha and Pseudepigrapha of the Old Testament*
BBB	Bonner biblische Beiträge
BDB	F. Brown, S. R. Driver, and C. A. Briggs, *Hebrew and English Lexicon of the Old Testament*
BETL	Bibliotheca ephemeridum theologicarum lovaniensium
BZAW	Beihefte zur ZAW
CBQ	*Catholic Biblical Quarterly*
CBQMS	Catholic Biblical Quarterly—Monograph Series
DTC	*Dictionnaire de théologie catholique*
EHAT	Exegetisches Handbuch zum Alten Testament
ET	English translation
HNT	Handbuch zum Neuen Testament
HUCA	*Hebrew Union College Annual*
ICC	International Critical Commentary
IDB	G. A. Buttrick (ed.), *Interpreter's Dictionary of the Bible*
JAOS	*Journal of the American Oriental Society*
JBL	*Journal of Biblical Literature*
LCL	Loeb Classical Library
OLZ	*Orientalische Literaturzeitung*
RB	*Revue biblique*
RSR	*Recherches de science religieuse*
RSV	*Revised Standard Version*
RTL	*Revue théologique de Louvain*
SBT	Studies in Biblical Theology
SVTP	Studia in Veteris Testamenti pseudepigrapha
TDNT	G. Kittel and G. Friedrich (eds.), *Theological Dictionary of the New Testament*
TLZ	*Theologische Literaturzeitung*
VT	*Vetus Testamentum*
WMANT	Wissenschaftliche Monographien zum Alten und Neuen Testament
ZAW	*Zeitschrift für die alttestamentliche Wissenschaft*
ZTK	*Zeitschrift für Theologie und Kirche*

FOREWORD

The following study is the result of that happy by-product that often issues from research: an accidental discovery. During the academic year 1976-1977 I was on a sabbatical leave in Claremont studying ethics in Hellenistic Judaism, and I found myself more and more engaged by the challenges to understanding posed by Ben Sira. After I had noted a few references in the scholarly literature on Ben Sira, and on Jewish wisdom generally, to Demotic wisdom literature—especially Berend Gemser's "The Instructions of 'Onchsheshonqy and Biblical Wisdom Literature," reprinted in James L. Crenshaw (ed.), *Studies in Ancient Israelite Wisdom*—I realized that the Demotic wisdom literature might help to provide some context for understanding Ben Sira, and so I began to examine it. 'Onchsheshonqy I found interesting, albeit not exciting, but it was when I sat down with a copy of František Lexa's edition and translation of *Papyrus Insinger* that I was struck, even startled, by the degree to which the author of *Insinger* seemed to have had many of the same ideas that Ben Sira also expressed, including the ethics of caution so characteristic of Ben Sira, and to have expressed those ideas in terms similar to Ben Sira's. *Papyrus Insinger* therefore posed the questions: Exactly how close was this apparent relationship, and how was it to be explained? The present monograph is my attempt to answer those questions.

Naturally, no study of this nature can be made without the help of many persons, and I should like here to thank those who have had the most to do directly with my work. The people without whom this study would have been totally impossible are the interlibrary loan librarians who have been so constantly willing to be of service, and I should like to thank Mrs. Jean L. Cobb of the School of Theology at Claremont, and Joanne Halgren and her staff at the University of Oregon for outstanding assistance. It was the leisure of a sabbatical year, of course, which provided the first opportunity for this study (Ben Sira: "The wisdom of the scribe *cometh by opportunity of leisure*"), and I must certainly thank the Oregon State System of Higher Education for making the sabbatical year available to me, as well as the Society of Biblical Literature, which awarded me one of the first of the SBL fellowships. Also, I should like to offer special thanks to Professor James M. Robinson, Director, and his staff at the Institute for Antiquity and Christianity for providing office space and many other amenities during that sabbatical year. Two prominent scholars in the field of wisdom studies, Professor James L. Crenshaw and Professor Robert Gordis, very generously took time from pressing schedules to read through the manuscript in earlier stages of its preparation and to offer numerous helpful suggestions and criticisms. I have profited greatly from their advice and acknowledge my gratitude to them, although I must confess that I have not taken all their advice, so that errors of judgment that may appear on the following pages will have to be placed to my own account. I wish also to thank Professor Crenshaw for accepting the manuscript for publication in the SBL Monograph Series. My wife, Susan E. Plass, in addition to providing the loving support and encouragement for which spouses are customarily thanked on pages such as this, has also prepared the indexes, for which I am indeed most grateful. Finally, my grateful thanks to the several typists at the University of Oregon who have labored with great skill over sometimes almost impossible copy to turn this work into a beautifully finished manuscript: Judith Gall, Sandy Livingston, Vicki Van Nortwick, and Elizabeth Mills.

Jack T. Sanders
Dept. of Religious Studies
University of Oregon
21 December 1981

INTRODUCTION

INTERNATIONAL HELLENISM

The Hellenistic Age was the ancient world's first truly international period. With the promotion and adoption not only of the Greek language, but also of Greek learning, Greek architecture, and even Greek lifestyles throughout the vast area originally conquered by Alexander, people lived in "one world" to a greater degree than had been the case even during the period of the "pax persiana."[1] Thus, for example, the founder of the Stoic school of philosophy, Zeno, was from Cyprus and apparently a Semite, and his successor leaders of the school for several generations came from the east: Chrysippus ("probably from Tarsus"),[2] Zeno of Tarsus, Diogenes of Babylon, Antipater of Tarsus, Archedemus of Tarsus, and Boethus of Sidon.[3] On the other side, the Jewish historian Josephus could refer with familiarity to the works of such older Greek writers as Anaxagoras and Plato,[4] while the Alexandrian Jewish philosopher Philo reflects everywhere the concepts of Platonism and could draw on Pythagorean principles to help explain the rationale for the Sabbath.[5]

Because of this recognized Hellenistic internationalism in learning, the modern scholar seeking to understand a writer of that period will wish perforce to identify strands of traditional ideas and themes continued, employed, or reinterpreted by the ancient writer, as well as intrusions of foreign elements, as an aid to understanding his work and his thinking. This is not to suggest that the student should indulge in what Samuel Sandmel so aptly called "parallelomania,"[6] but rather to propose that, in the identification of the traditions utilized by a particular writer and in the analysis of the *way* in which he used them, one may gain a richer appreciation of the unique contribution of that writer. Such a task is here to be undertaken. It is the purpose of this study to shed further light on one identifiable strand of tradition in Ben Sira that has not received adequate

[1] Cf. M. Hadas, *Hellenistic Culture. Fusion and Diffusion* (New York and London: Columbia University Press, 1959).

[2] Ibid., 107.

[3] Ibid., 106–7.

[4] Josephus *Ag.Ap.* 2.168.

[5] *Op.* 102.

[6] S. Sandmel, "Parallelomania," *JBL* 81 (1962) 1–13.

clarification heretofore—namely, Egyptian wisdom of the Ptolemaic period—and, in so doing, to reach a more adequate definition of the thinking of this erudite and thoughtful ancient sage.

CHAPTER 1

BEN SIRA'S RELATION TO JUDAIC TRADITION

The Proverbial Wisdom Tradition

The student who wishes to acquire an adequate understanding of Ben Sira, whether of the various themes which interact within his work or of the influences which acted upon him, must first have in mind the nature and extent of Ben Sira's relation to the continuing Judaic wisdom tradition—the degree to which he drew, so to speak, from the same stream from which the authors of the Book of Proverbs drew.[1] To what degree is Ben Sira anticipated by those earlier authors? To what extent is his collected wisdom—the crowning extant achievement of the Judaic proverbial wisdom tradition—simply the continuation of their themes or even of their maxims? If one is to reach a clear perspective specifically on our author's "Egyptian connection"—the possible influence on him of certain Egyptian wisdom documents—one must first understand the ways in which and the extent to which he has carried on the inherited traditions of his own people.

So numerous and obvious, in fact, are the connections between Ben Sira and the older proverbial tradition that one commentator, Paul Volz, in his commentary in the *Schriften des Alten Testaments* series, did not distinguish Ben Sira from Proverbs for the purpose of analysis, but rather considered the two together, grouping proverbs from both works together in thematic units.[2] It will thus be convenient simply to follow

---

[1] The Book of Proverbs is not, of course, coterminous with the Judaic wisdom tradition; but one will recall that Proverbs and Ben Sira belong together as the only surviving exemplars of the "normal" or "conventional" or even "lower" wisdom that was the didactic presentation of collections of proverbs. Job, Qoheleth, and the Wisdom of Solomon—as "theological" or "unconventional" or "higher" wisdom works—are to be understood only against the background of the "conventional" tradition. On this point cf. R. Gordis, *Koheleth—the Man and His World. A Study of Ecclesiastes* (3d ed.; New York: Schocken, 1968) 25-26. Gordis refers to Proverbs and Ben Sira as the "major documents" of the "main school of Wisdom." Ben Sira was of course aware of Job and of Qoheleth, on which relationship cf. further below.

[2] P. Volz, *Hiob und Weisheit* (Die Schriften des Alten Testaments 3/2; 2d ed.; Göttingen: Vandenhoeck & Ruprecht, 1921). For a complete study of the relation of Ben Sira to Judaic tradition, which is quite beyond the scope of this work, one will also wish to

Volz in noting the way in which Ben Sira continues the older wisdom, as it is deposited in the book of Proverbs.[3]

One may begin by observing an obvious formal similarity, especially between Proverbs 1–9, the latest section of the Book of Proverbs, and Ben Sira. In both collections one finds a development beyond mere collections of elaborated proverbs, as in the older sections of Proverbs, to conceptually unified discourses built up from proverbial statements. Thus, simply to begin at the beginning of each book, Prov 1:2–7 explains the purpose of the book to be the offering of wisdom to all and connects this wisdom with the fear of Yahweh, and Sir 1:1–10 extols the eternal wisdom, which is then, in 1:11–20, equated systematically with the fear of the Lord. This formal observation, therefore, brings us to the first material similarity between the two collections, namely the equation of traditional wisdom with the (Deuteronomic) fear of Yahweh. If the collection of Proverbs 1–9 includes at the beginning (1:7) and at the end (9:10) the tenet that the fear of Yahweh is the beginning of knowledge or of wisdom, it is this tenet which is expanded poetically by Ben Sira in Sir 1:14, 16, 18, and 20, where he equates the fear of the Lord with the beginning, the fullness, the crown, and the root of wisdom.[4] While the Hebrew text for these verses of Ben Sira is not extant, it would appear that Sir 1:14a is actually a quotation of Ps 111:10 (so Segal),[5] which is of course related to the wisdom tradition of Prov 1:7 and 9:10.

Again, in their expressions of the traditional sage view of the inevitableness of recompense for folly, there seems to be a direct relation between Ben Sira and the older collections. Prov 26:27 advises, "He who digs a pit will fall into it, and a stone will come back upon him who

---

consult, in addition to the commentaries, T. Middendorp, *Die Stellung Jesu Ben Siras zwischen Judentum und Hellenismus* (Leiden: Brill, 1973) 51–91.

[3] The translation of Proverbs followed here is that of the Revised Standard Version of the Bible; the translation of Ben Sira is that of G. H. Box and W. O. E. Oesterley in *APOT* 1 (1913). In some cases, examination of the Hebrew of Proverbs or of the Hebrew, Greek, and Syriac of Ben Sira has led me to alter the translation followed, and these alterations appear in italics. If, in such cases, a person familiar with the texts might be uncertain as to what text I am reading, I give it in the notes; and, if an emendation is involved, I supply a brief explanation. For Ben Sira, the critical Hebrew text published by F. Vattioni, *Ecclesiastico. Testo ebraico con apparato critico e versioni greca, latina e siriaca* (Testi 1; Naples: Istituto orientale di Napoli, 1968)—and, where the Hebrew text is not extant, the Ziegler Greek text, printed by Vattioni—are generally preferred throughout to the restored text read by Box and Oesterley, although I have not emended Box and Oesterley's English translation to bring it into conformity with the Vattioni text when the differences have appeared insignificant. I have, also, always transliterated *yhwh* as Yahweh, regardless of what appears in the translation being followed.

I have, here, always cited the verse enumerations of the Box and Oesterley ET of Ben Sira and of the RSV for the Bible.

[4] Volz, *Hiob und Weisheit*, 119.

[5] M. Ṣ. Sgl, *Spr Bn Syr' Haššlm* (Yrwšlym: Mwsd By'lyq, 1958).

starts it rolling," and Sir 27:25a, 26a repeats the theme and the figure: "He that casteth a stone on high casteth it on his own head, . . . He that diggeth a pit shall fall into it."[6] The theme of death, further, as the final recompense for the evil persons who have prospered in life, appears frequently in Ben Sira, but Sir 9:11–12, "Envy not the *wicked* man, For thou knowest not what his destiny shall be. Envy not the arrogant man that prospereth, Remember that he shall not escape unpunished till death," appears to be a close variant of Prov 24:19–20: "Fret not yourself because of evildoers, and be not envious of the wicked; for the evil man has no future; the lamp of the wicked will be put out."[7] Further, the identification that is found everywhere in Ben Sira between sin and folly, righteousness and wisdom, is also to be found in Proverbs. An example is Sir 27:8, where the advice, "If thou follow after righteousness, thou wilt attain, And put it on as a robe of glory," intends the pursuit of righteousness as practical advice, as the setting makes clear. (We may note, for example, the following advice in v 11, "The discourse of the *pious* man continueth in wisdom, But the fool changeth as the moon.") One may therefore see that the "glory" which can be "attained" by the "pursuit" of righteousness is of the same order as the glory which is attained in the pursuit of wisdom. Righteousness, in other words, is sage—a view which is also to be found frequently in Proverbs, e.g., in 14:16: "A wise man is *fearful* and turns away from evil."[8] Consequently, to fear God is also sage in both works, as we may note in Sir 40:26b: "In the fear of Yahweh there is no want, And with it there is no need to seek support"; or Prov 22:4: "The *consequence of* humility *is* fear of Yahweh, riches and honor and life."[9]

Both Proverbs and Ben Sira endorse prudential silence. Thus Prov 25:7c, 8 advise: "What your eyes have seen do not hastily bring into court"; and Sir 19:10 admonishes similarly: "Hast thou heard something? let it die with thee."[10] Both also, naturally, remark on the advantages of wisdom over folly. Thus Sir 20:30 refers to "hidden wisdom and concealed treasure," and 22:7 explains that "He who teacheth a fool is (as) one that glueth together a potsherd," whereas Prov 17:12 offers the comparison: "Let a man meet a *bereaved bear* rather than a fool in his folly."[11] A mark of folly is arrogant pride, and the famous proverb, "Pride goes before destruction, and a haughty spirit before a fall" (Prov 16:18), finds its echo in Sir 10:7–8: "Pride is hateful to the Lord and to men, And before both oppression is an offence. Sovereignty is transferred from nation to nation

---

6 Volz, *Hiob und Weisheit*, 147; cf. also Qoh 10:8–9.

7 Cf. also Ps 37:1.

8 Cf. Volz, *Hiob und Weisheit*, 164.

9 Ibid., 167.

10 Ibid., 179.

11 Ibid., 185.

On account of the violence of pride."[12]

Regarding private life, both Proverbs and Ben Sira cite a fortunate marriage as an advantage. Prov 18:22 states that "He who finds a wife finds a good thing, and obtains favor from Yahweh"; and Ben Sira endorses a very similar sentiment when he affirms that "A good wife (is) a good gift: She shall be given to him that feareth *Yahweh*, for his portion" (Sir 26:3).[13] For sons, both advise a rigid rearing. Thus Prov 13:24: "He who spares the rod hates his son, but he who loves him is diligent to *train* him"; and Sir 30:2, 13: "He that *traineth* his son shall have satisfaction of him, And among his acquaintance glory in him. . . . *Train* thy son and make his yoke heavy, Lest in his folly he stumble."[14]

On the subject of neighborliness, the admonition of Prov 25:17, "Let your foot be seldom in your neighbor's house, lest he become *sated with you and hate you*," appears to be reiterated in Sir 21:22–23 (following Box and Oesterley's line rearrangement): "The foot of a fool hasteth into a house, But *a well trained man will* stand outside."[15]

Quite close to each other are Proverbs and Ben Sira in their remarks concerning the differences to be observed between the station in life of the rich and that of the poor. Aside from Prov 10:15, "A rich man's wealth is his strong city; the poverty of the poor is their ruin," three proverbs on the same theme occur in near proximity to one another in Prov 18:23; 19:4, and 6: "The poor use entreaties, but the rich answer roughly. . . . Wealth brings many new friends, but a poor man is deserted by his friend. . . . Many seek the favor of a generous man, and every one is a friend to a man who gives gifts." Alongside these sayings one may place two short sections in Ben Sira, Sir 13:21–23 and 31:1–4:[16]

> A rich man when he is shaken is supported by a friend,
>> But the poor man when he is shaken is thrust *from friend to* friend.
> A rich man speaketh, and his helpers are many;
>> And his *hateful* words *are made beautiful.*
> A poor man *is shaken*, and they jeer at him;
>> Yea, though he speak with wisdom, there is no place for him.
> When the rich man speaketh, all keep silence,
>> And they extol his intelligence to the clouds.

[12] Ibid., 187.

[13] Ibid., 190.

[14] Ibid., 194. Here and elsewhere I have consistently translated *ysr/mwsr* as "train/training." While this English word is still not a perfect translation, it seems to me best to carry the nuances of the Hebrew word, which are expressed both in the generally preferred "discipline" and in the "instruction" of the RSV.

[15] Volz, *Hiob und Weisheit*, 215.

[16] Ibid., 198; cf. also Qoh 9:16.

When the poor man speaketh: "Who is this?" say they:
And if he stumble they will assist his overthrow.

Deception over wealth wasteth *his* flesh;
Anxiety about *sustenance hindereth* slumber.
Anxiety about sustenance breaketh off slumber,
Even as severe sickness *hindereth slumber*.
The rich man laboureth to gather riches,
And when he resteth, it is to *gather* delights.
The poor man toileth for the needs of his house,
And *when* he *resteth* he becometh needy.

Similarly, the proverb in Prov 18:24 about both possibilities of friendship—
"There are friends who pretend to be friends, but there is a friend who
sticks closer than a brother"—readily calls to mind the section on
friendship in Sir 6:5–17, especially vv 8 and 16: "There is a friend (who is
so) according to occasion, And continueth not in the day of *distress*; . . . A
faithful friend is a 'bundle of life,' He that feareth God *attaineth them*."[17]

Prov 16:31, "A hoary head is a crown of glory; it is gained in a
righteous life," would appear to be picked up and slightly reworked in Sir
25:6, "The crown of the aged is their much experience, And their glorying
is the fear of the Lord."[18]

Again, Prov 21:3, "To do righteousness and justice is more acceptable
to Yahweh than sacrifice," appears to be expanded in Sir 35:1–9, a section
that deals with the same theme. One may note especially v 1, "He that
keepeth the law multiplieth offerings; He sacrificeth a peace-offering that
heedeth the commandments"; and v 9, "In all thy deeds let thy
countenance shine, And with gladness dedicate thy tithe."[19] Further, the
theme of Prov 15:8, "The sacrifice of the wicked is an abomination to
Yahweh, but the prayer of the upright is his delight," may be taken over
and altered somewhat in Sir 35:3: "A thing well-pleasing to the Lord it is to
avoid wickedness, And a propitiation to avoid what is wrong."[20] Perhaps a
still more striking similarity is found in the proverbs in both works about
the effect of righteousness on the state. Sir 16:4, "From *a childless* one that
feareth Yahweh a city is peopled, But through a race of treacherous men it
is desolated," appears to be merely a variant of Prov 11:11: "By the blessing
of the upright a city is exalted, but it is overthrown by the mouth of the
wicked."[21]

---

[17] Volz, *Hiob und Weisheit*, 206.
[18] Ibid., 209. While the Hebrew of Sir 25:6 is not extant, the similarity to Prov 16:31 was
seen by Segal, who rendered *stephanos* by '*trh* and *kauchēma* by *tp'rh*, the same words
for "crown" and "glory" as appear in Prov 16:31; and Ben Sira's "fear of the Lord" is
comparable to the "righteousness" of Proverbs.
[19] Volz, *Hiob und Weisheit*, 213.
[20] Ibid.
[21] Ibid., 221.

On the propriety of giving alms to the poor, Proverbs and Ben Sira are, of course, in agreement (as was the entire Ancient Near East).[22] Thus Prov 3:27–28 advises, "Do not withhold good from those to whom it is due, when it is in your power to do it. Do not say to your neighbor, 'Go, and come again, tomorrow I will give it'—when you have it with you"; and likewise Sir 4:1–5:

> My son, defraud not the poor of his sustenance,
>> And grieve not the *soul of the poor* that is bitter in (his) soul.
> Despise not the needy soul,[23]
>> And turn not away from the *oppressed* soul.[24]
> *Do not cause the intestines* of the oppressed *to be in a ferment,*
>> And *do not pain the inward parts of the poor.*
> Withhold not a gift from *your* poor.
> *And* despise not the supplication of the poor,
>> And give him none occasion to curse thee.[25]

Finally, in both works one finds encouragement of the proper (cautious, humble) approach to princes and kings when in their service. Prov 25:6–7 advises, "Do not *claim honor* in the king's presence or stand in the place of the great; for it is better to be told, 'Come up here,' than to be put lower in the presence of the prince"; and Ben Sira perhaps revises the very saying when he cautions, "Doth a noble draw near? keep at a distance—And so much the more will he cause thee to approach. Do not thyself draw near, lest thou be put at a distance; And keep not (too) far away lest *thou be hated*" (Sir 13:9–10).[26]

Volz's compendium of proverbial topics does not, in fact, exhaust the range of relationships between Proverbs and Ben Sira. On occasion, one can even combine evidence from both works to see the way in which the Jewish sages worked over a particular idea or admonition proverbially in several stages. An example of this process at work is the variations on Prov 13:3, "He who guards his mouth preserves his life" (*nōṣēr pîw šōmēr napšô*), that occur in the second collection of the Book of Proverbs and in Ben Sira. Prov 16:17 advises that "he who guards his way preserves his life" (*šōmēr napšô nōṣēr darkô*), and Prov 19:16 that "he

---

[22] On this point cf. H. Bolkestein, *Wohltätigkeit und Armenpflege im vorchristlichen Altertum* (Groningen: Bouma, 1967). It was Bolkestein's accomplishment to show that peoples in the ANE conceived of care for the needy in terms of the rich aiding the poor (thus almsgiving), whereas the Greeks and Romans thought more in terms of demonstrating service to fellow human beings. Cf. in particular p. 441.

[23] The meaning of the Hebrew line is not clear.

[24] Reading *mimědukdak* for *mmdkdy*.

[25] Volz, *Hiob und Weisheit*, 224.

[26] Cf. Volz, *Hiob und Weisheit*, 228. Volz indicates a number of other equivalent themes in Ben Sira and the Book of Proverbs, but the similarities are less clear than in the instances given here.

who keeps the commandment keeps his life" (*šōmēr miṣwâ šōmēr napšô*). The last is then varied in Sir 32:24, "He that observeth the Law guardeth himself" (*nôṣēr tôrâ šōmēr napšô*)—whereby one notes that Ben Sira now thinks of the Torah and not merely of the instruction or admonition of the sage—but Prov 21:23 provides a playful variant of the proverb, the humor of which can be appreciated only in Hebrew: "He who keeps his mouth and his tongue keeps himself out of trouble" (*šōmēr pîw ûlĕšônô šōmēr miṣṣārôt napšô*).[27]

Another subject on which Proverbs and Ben Sira agree is women. "For the authors of Proverbs," wrote Robert Gordis some years ago, "there are three types of women: the temptress . . . , the quarrelsome wife . . . and finally, the ideal wife, or woman of valor."[28] Gordis then showed that these same ideas occur also in Ben Sira, and he cited, among other proverbs, the following: Prov 5:3–4, "The lips of a *strange* woman drip honey, and her speech is smoother than oil; but in the end she is bitter as wormwood"; 21:9, "It is better to live in a corner of the housetop than in a house shared with a contentious woman"; 31:10–31, "A *strong* wife who can find? Her price is above that of corals," etc.; and the section Sir 26:1–27, where all three themes interact. We may note particularly vv 11–12, where Ben Sira warns of the "headstrong daughter" (v 10):

> Look well after a shameless eye,
>   And marvel not if it trespass against thee.
> As a thirsty traveller that openeth his mouth,
>   And drinketh of any water that is near,
> So she sitteth down at every post,
>   And openeth [her] quiver to *an* arrow,

and v 26a: "The woman that honoureth her own husband appeareth wise unto all, But she that dishonoureth (her husband) is known to all as one that is godless in (her) pride."

Most students of Ben Sira have noted his "eudaemonism"—his interest in success and a happy or fortunate life. Volz referred to Ben Sira's "certain egoistic coldness" in this regard[29] and observed that the "motive of all dealing" was "that one become fortunate, advance, never

---

[27] The student sage, accustomed to hearing and repeating proverbs like Prov 13:3; 16:17; and especially 19:16, will have correctly heard the beginning of Prov 21:23 as another variant of the same proverb, with the first stich expanded to include "and his tongue," a reasonable addition to the keeping of the mouth. Upon hearing the beginning, however, of the word *mṣrwt* ("out of trouble"), the student will have expected *mṣwh* ("the commandment"). The surprise, then, of the substituted word, coupled with its somewhat lighter theme ("himself out of trouble" instead of the more serious "himself" or "his life") provides the moment of humor.

[28] R. Gordis, "The Social Background of Wisdom Literature," *HUCA* 18 (1944) 111.

[29] Volz, *Hiob und Weisheit*, 174.

suffer sorrow, [and] be able to live and to die peacefully."[30] The
observation is widely repeated in the literature.[31] While many authors at
least imply, however, that this trait is highly characteristic of Ben Sira if
not even relatively unique, Crawford H. Toy, in his commentary on the
Book of Proverbs, already called attention to the similarity between Ben
Sira and the Book of Proverbs on this point. "*Proverbs* and *Ben Sira*," he
wrote, "confine themselves to cheery practical suggestions for the
conduct of every-day life."[32]

If Ben Sira, therefore, counsels in 15:15–17,

> If thou (so) desirest, thou canst keep the commandment,
>   *And if thou trust in him, of a truth thou shalt live.*[33]
> Poured out before thee (are) fire and water,
>   Stretch forth thine hand unto that which thou desirest.
> Life and death (are) before man,
>   That which he desireth shall be given to him,

or if he advises (30:22) that "Heart-joy is life for a man, And human
gladness *postpones anger*," or if he states as a principle (30:15), "*A life
of* soundness have I desired more than fine gold, And a cheerful spirit
more than *corals*," he is really doing nothing more than continuing the
eudaemonistic tradition of the Book of Proverbs.

Life as motivation for or result of sage behavior, as a matter of fact,
occurs in the Book of Proverbs no fewer than twenty-five times, of

---

30 Ibid., 107.

31 Cf., e.g., O. F. Fritzsche, *Kurzgefasstes exegetisches Handbuch zu den Apokryphen
des Alten Testamentes*. Fünfte Lieferung: *Die Weisheit Jesus–Sirach's* (Leipzig:
S. Hirzel, 1859) xxxiv; L. Couard, *Die religiösen und sittlichen Anschauungen der
alttestamentlichen Apokryphen und Pseudepigraphen* (Gütersloh: Bertelsmann, 1909)
155; D. Michaelis, "Das Buch Jesus Sirach als typischer Ausdruck für das Gottesverhältnis
des nachalttestamentlichen Menschen," *TLZ* 83 (1958) 607; J. C. Rylaarsdam, *Revelation
in Jewish Wisdom Literature* (Chicago: Univ. of Chicago Press, 1946) 57–58; R. H.
Pfeiffer, *History of New Testament Times with an Introduction to the Apocrypha* (New
York: Harper, 1949) 386–92; H. M. Hughes, *The Ethics of Jewish Aprocryphal Literature*
(London: Robert Culley, s.d. [1910]) 38–39; V. Ryssel, "Die Sprüche Jesus', des Sohnes
Sirachs," *Die Apokryphen und Pseudepigraphen des Alten Testaments* 1: *Die
Apokryphen des Alten Testaments* (ed. E. Kautzsch; Tübingen: Mohr [Siebeck], 1900)
231; and E. G. Bauckmann, "Die Proverbien und die Sprüche des Jesus Sirach," *ZAW* 72
(1960) 47.

32 C. H. Toy, *A Critical and Exegetical Commentary on the Book of Proverbs* (ICC;
New York: Scribner's, 1908) xix.

33 Verse 15 has three stichoi, an anomaly. The translation given follows the Syriac,
which omits what is for the Hebrew the second stich, *ûtĕbûnâ la'ăśôt rĕṣônô*, which Box
and Oesterley take in preference to the stich retained above. They apparently thought
(although they do not so state) that their reading was supported by the Greek, but the
second line of the verse there, *kai pistin poiēsai eudokias*, appears rather to be a
compromise reading incorporating parts of both the stichoi in question. The reading
chosen here seems better to fit the context, cf. v 17.

which occurrences one may note especially Prov 10:17, "*The path of life is the keeping of training,*" and 13:14, "The teaching of the wise *man* is a fountain of life."[34] Ben Sira and the Book of Proverbs are thus in agreement on the importance of (the good) life.

The evidence here presented of similar themes and proverbs in the Book of Proverbs and in Ben Sira has not exhausted the topic of the relationship between the two works, but it has served, one may hope, to focus attention on at least the most obvious parallels and similarities. Perhaps it will serve the purpose of scholarly analysis to reflect briefly at this point on the meaning of such similarities for the understanding of Ben Sira.

The sages were, before anything else, tradents.[35] That which was true was passed on, an aspect of wisdom that at once set it in opposition to prophecy—which always listened for the word of God anew—and made it the forerunner of what we today call science. It was wisdom's function to *accumulate truth.*[36] Thus Gordis has referred to the "unconventional Wise Men," i.e., the authors of Job and Qoheleth, who, in their "role of teachers of Wisdom . . . probably contributed original sayings of their own, which were not different in form or spirit from that of their more conventional colleagues," the authors of Proverbs and Ben Sira.[37] Such a statement, of course, implies that the sayings of Proverbs and Ben Sira were conventional, and it is this "conventionality" which we see in the relationships between the Book of Proverbs and Ben Sira in the examples adduced above.[38] The most obvious place to locate Ben Sira, therefore, along the spectrum of Hellenistic intellectual activity, is solidly in the Judaic *proverbial* tradition.

Gerhard von Rad even thought that he found several examples of "school questions,"[39] the existence of which, of course, would attest the

---

[34] For further examples from Proverbs and from Ben Sira, cf. my article "Ben Sira's Ethics of Caution," *HUCA* 50 (1980) 73–106.

[35] Cf. also J. L. Crenshaw, *Old Testament Wisdom. An Introduction* (Atlanta: John Knox, 1981) 42.

[36] This is not to overlook the fact that there were also prophetic traditions. Thus Isaiah and Micah could take up Amos's appeal for social justice, and Jeremiah could employ Hosea's familial figures of speech. Nevertheless, the prophet was not an accumulator of traditional wisdom, as was the sage, in spite of a certain tendency within recent scholarship to collapse the differences between the two. In this latter vein, cf. J. L. Crenshaw, "*eṣā* and *dabar*: The Problem of Authority/Certitude in Wisdom and Prophetic Literature," *Prophetic Conflict. Its Effect Upon Israelite Religion* (BZAW 124; Berlin & New York: de Gruyter, 1971) 116–23 and the literature referred to there.

[37] R. Gordis, "Quotations in Wisdom Literature," *Studies in Ancient Israelite Wisdom* (ed. James L. Crenshaw; New York: KTAV, 1976) 222. Cf. further above, n. 1.

[38] Ryssel, "Jesus Sirach," 231, went so far as to say that there was no foreign influence at all in Ben Sira. Similarly also N. Peters, *Das Buch Jesus Sirach oder Ecclesiasticus* (EHAT 25; Münster in Westf.: Aschendorff, 1913) XXXVIII.

[39] G. von Rad, *Wisdom in Israel* (Nashville and N.Y.: Abingdon, 1972) 18–19. Crenshaw, *Wisdom*, 163–64, notes questions as a literary device in Ben Sira and does not

accumulative and conventional nature of wisdom. Von Rad cited, among other texts, Prov 23:29–30: "Who has woe? Who has *pain*? Who has strife? Who has complaining? Who has wounds without cause? Who has *dullness* of eyes? Those who tarry long over wine, those who go to *seek* mixed wine"; and Ps 34:12–13: "What man is there who desires life, *who loves [many] days*, that he may enjoy good? Keep your tongue from evil, and your lips from speaking deceit." In addition, of course, von Rad referred to the advertisement in Sir 51:23 mentioning the "house of instruction"[40] and to Sir 39:1–11, "an ideal portrait of a scholar and teacher of the time of Sirach."[41] In this last passage reference is made to the one "who searcheth out the wisdom of all the ancients And is occupied with the prophets; Who heedeth the discourses of men of renown, And entereth into the deep things of parables; Searcheth out the hidden meaning of proverbs, And is conversant with the dark saying of parables; . . . Who travelleth through the lands of *other* peoples."[42]

The matter is clear. Ben Sira considered it his function to examine the wisdom of the ancients and of his contemporaries, and to accumulate and to hand on such wisdom as he found worthwhile, offering new insight as he deemed it warranted or necessary.[43] Furthermore, he tells us plainly that he is no narrow provincial, but that he gives consideration to the wisdom of his own countrymen and of others, *wherever that may be found*. We are thus not surprised to have found the wisdom of the Book of Proverbs in Ben Sira, but it is the *wherever* that has attracted our attention, and we thus now turn to a consideration of what might be termed the "non-Proverbial remainder" of Ben Sira—those aspects of his work which are *not* the transmission of conventional Judaic proverbial wisdom.

Divergencies from Proverbial Wisdom Characteristics

One of the first differences that one notes is that the work has a named author. The author gives his name in 50:27, although the manuscript evidence is not clear as to whether his name was Simeon or

---

refer to schools. Regarding the question of the Israelite wisdom school generally, one may wish to consult further H.-J. Hermisson, *Studien zur israelitischen Spruchweisheit* (WMANT 28; Neukirchen-Vluyn: Neukirchener Verlag, 1968) 97–133; B. Lang, *Frau Weisheit: Deutung einer biblischen Gestalt* (Düsseldorf: Patmos, 1975); and *idem*, "Schule und Unterricht im alten Israel," *La Sagesse de l'Ancien Testament* (BETL 51; ed. M. Gilbert; Gembloux: Duculot, 1979) 186–201.

40 Von Rad, *Wisdom in Israel*, 17.

41 Ibid., 22.

42 One may note also especially Sir 24:30–31.

43 Gordis, *Koheleth*, 43, referred to Qoheleth's "*creative use of traditional material*, his giving to the time-hallowed texts a meaning congenial to his own unconventional religious outlook." Save for the word "unconventional" this statement applies to Ben Sira as well.

Yeshua and whether he was the great-grandson or grandson of Sira. Among the non-prophetic books in the ancient Judaic tradition, this naming of the author is quite remarkable (assuming that the word Qoheleth is what it appears to be and not a name). Furthermore, the book has a conscious order, or at least a climax (since the attempt at order is clearer at the end than elsewhere). As the book now stands, an opening praise of Wisdom (1:1-20) is followed by a miscellany of advice sections, but the long end of the book is rounded off in a conscious sequence of parts. The body concludes with the climactic 41:12-13:[44] "Be in fear for thy name, for that abideth longer for thee Than thousands of treasures *of wisdom. The value of* a life lasts for *a number of* days, But the *value* of a name for days without number," a pair of proverbs that summarizes the main point of the book. Then follows, in 41:14-42:8, what Josef Haspecker has called a "doubled decalogue about shame reiterating the main points of the book"[45]—that is, a nutshell formulation of Ben Sira's advice spelling out the truth of 41:12-13. There follow, then, a few proverbs thrown in about the problems daughters cause; while this collection of proverbs is related to the summary statement of 41:14-42:8, it lacks its summary character and appears to be an afterthought. Next, however, in 42:15-43:33, Ben Sira praises Yahweh as the lord of nature. The point of this section is that Yahweh is revealed in nature and that his wisdom is available to all, which is in fact said in the concluding proverb of the section: "Everything [hath Yahweh made], And to [the pious hath He given wisdom]." Following this, 44:1 begins the long "Praise of the Fathers," which extends down to 50:24. Here is no *Heilsgeschichte*, but rather a paean on the fame and glory of bygone Jewish heroes and, finally, of one contemporary. The rationale given for this long section in 44:8, "Some of them there are who have left a name, *That men might tell of it in their inheritance*," shows the connection Ben Sira sees with the climactic theme of 41:12-13.[46] The book then concludes in 50:27-29, following the brief embarassing statement about the foreigners Ben Sira hates.[47] Chap. 51 is an appendix.

---

[44] So also, essentially, R. Smend, *Die Weisheit des Jesus Sirach* (Berlin: Georg Reimer, 1906) XXIV–XXV.

[45] J. Haspecker, *Gottesfurcht bei Jesus Sirach. Ihre religiöse Struktur und ihre literarische und doktrinäre Bedeutung* (AnBib 30; Rome: Pontificio Instituto Biblico, 1967) 185.

[46] The rationale proposed by R. T. Siebeneck, "May Their Bones Return to Life!—Sirach's Praise of the Fathers," *CBQ* 21 (1959) 411-28, for the Praise of the Fathers, that the section is an apologetic against Hellenism, extolling Hebraic features, has no textual support. It was Smend, of course, who first proposed this understanding of the section.

[47] Ryssel, "Jesus Sirach," 240, also saw the more pronounced structure in the latter part of the work. Cf. also Peters, *Jesus Sirach*, XXXIX.

This description of the concluding sections of Ben Sira reveals that there is a conscious order extending over the final ten chapters or approximately one-fifth of the book,[48] the purpose of which organization is to emphasize that God has revealed his wisdom, by precept and example, copiously and at great length, so that everyone might acquire "the *value* of a name" which is "for days without number." The Jewish proverbial tradition prior to Ben Sira attests no such organization of several large units into an over-all scheme,[49] although Qoheleth, indeed, moves in this direction. As Gordis notes, the "Allegory of Old Age" (Qoh 11:7–12:8) is "the climax and conclusion of the book." Even so, however, Qoheleth provides "no logical progression of thought . . . in the book," whereas we have seen that Ben Sira, in the final ten chapters, more nearly does so.[50]

In addition to this "grand order" at the end, organization of a somewhat different kind can be seen in Ben Sira, which again distinguishes it from the Book of Proverbs, or, at least, from the primary collection of proverbs in Proverbs 10–22 and 25–29. This is the organization of small units of material into something like chapters dealing with specific themes, a phenomenon which can be observed in the Book of Proverbs only in Proverbs 1–9, where various themes related to Wisdom are taken up in order, and in 31:10–31, the section on the good wife.[51] The difference between the Book of Proverbs and Ben Sira in this matter has already surfaced in the discussion above of their similarities, for there we saw that advice which appeared as one proverb in the Book of Proverbs might appear as an entire section in Ben Sira.[52] Thus Prov 13:24, on the training of a son, is echoed in Sir 30:1–13; and the individual proverbs in the Book of Proverbs pointing out the differences between the rich and the poor (Prov 10:15; 18:23; 19:4, 6) correspond to fairly lengthy sections in Ben Sira (Sir 13:21–23 and 31:1–4). A proverb

---

[48] Cf. also Smend, *Weisheit*, XXXVII.

[49] P. W. Skehan, in an essay entitled, "A Single Editor for the Whole Book of Proverbs," *Studies in Israelite Poetry and Wisdom* (CBQMS 1; Washington: Catholic Biblical Association of America, 1971) 15–26, has argued that a single editor or "compiler" (p. 18) is responsible for an "artificial external structure" (p. 20) that determines the number of proverbs in each collection in the Book of Proverbs as well as the total number of proverbs in the entire book. Even if this theory should prove to be true, and Skehan indicates its several problems, such a manner of determining number would not be the same as Ben Sira's conceptual organizing principle.

[50] Cf. Gordis, *Koheleth*, 110–11.

[51] The Words of Agur ben Yakeh, Prov 30:1–9, while dealing with one theme—scepticism and belief—should not be considered an example of thematic sections in the Book of Proverbs, since the section belongs to the general Ancient Near Eastern type of the sceptical dialogue.

[52] The proverbs and sections to which reference is here made have already been quoted above, pp. 6–9. Qoheleth, too, of course, organizes his proverbs into discourses or chapters.

on varieties of friendship (Prov 18:24), further, becomes in Ben Sira the substantial section Sir 6:5-17; and the same relationship is to be observed between Prov 21:3, on the relative value of righteousness and sacrifice, and Sir 35:1-9, where Ben Sira uses a much longer space to make essentially the same point. Proverbs about the propriety of almsgiving and care for the poor also experience a similar expansion between Prov 3:27-28, as was noted above, and Sir 4:1-5; and the advice in Prov 25:6-7 on proper behavior before royalty is answered in Ben Sira by a much lengthier section, Sir 13:8-13. Finally, the several themes about women, as in Prov 5:3-4; 21:9; and 31:10-31, are taken up in one unified section in Sir 26:1-27.

We thus see that Ben Sira has a pronounced tendency to organize his practical advice into groups of proverbs, thereby presenting the reader with discourses rather than with individual sayings.[53] To be sure, the latest section of the Book of Proverbs—chaps. 1-9—had also done this,[54] but there are still certain differences. Proverbs 1-9 is more theological discourse on hypostatized wisdom than it is practical advice (although practical advice does occur there), whereas we have seen that Ben Sira employs the expanded proverb-collection unit to present his practical advice. Thus one might say that Ben Sira has carried the altered form of wisdom writing of Proverbs 1-9, which is more theological than practical, over onto the content of traditional advice. Yet one more difference remains, and that is Ben Sira's tendency to round off these sections with final summary proverbs, a trait which is not to be observed in Proverbs 1-9.[55] Thus, for example, Ben Sira concludes a section on benevolence and almsgiving, 7:32-36, with v 36: "In all thy doings remember thy last end, Then wilt thou never do corruptly." A section on the value of forgiveness as opposed to vengeance, further (Sir 27:30-28:7), concludes similarly in 28:6: "Remember thy last end, and cease from enmity; (Remember) corruption and death, and abide in the commandments." The advice section in Sir 35:1-11 on the value of righteousness with regard to sacrifices draws to a close with v 10: "Give to God as He hath given to thee, With goodness of eye, and as thine hand hath attained"; and Sir 37:7-15, on true and false counselors ("hide thy counsel from him that is *zealous*," v 10, etc.), offers the following encompassing advice in conclusion (v 15): "In all this intreat God, That He may *establish* thy steps in truth." The trait is to be observed

---

[53] Crenshaw, *Wisdom*, 160, also notes this stylistic difference, as well as the general reliance of Ben Sira on older proverbial tradition.

[54] Cf. W. Fuss, "Tradition und Komposition im Buche Jesus Sirach" (Dissertation Tübingen, 1962) 275; Crenshaw, *Wisdom*, 149.

[55] Fuss, "Tradition und Komposition," 278-79, has indicated the following examples. Qoheleth, again, also draws conclusions. Crenshaw, *Wisdom*, 162-63, notes Ben Sira's use of "refrains."

frequently elsewhere, and one may therefore see that Ben Sira has attempted to organize his advice thematically in a way that is not characteristic of the Book of Proverbs, even of chaps. 1–9.

The next "non-proverbial" trait that one notices in Ben Sira is his identification of Wisdom with Torah. While the latest section of the Book of Proverbs, chaps. 1–9, had moved in the direction of an equation of the two, no writer before Ben Sira had quite taken the last step of identification. One can read in Prov 1:7 that "the fear of Yahweh is the beginning of knowledge" and in 9:10 "of wisdom," and one will surely recall the frequent Deuteronomic admonitions to the fear of Yahweh (cf., e.g., Deut 10:12) and the explanation of this admonition as keeping the commandments.[56] Yet Ben Sira makes the identification direct and explicit. In 19:20 he asserts, "All wisdom is the fear of the Lord, And *in* all wisdom is the *doing* of the Law"; and, at the end of the praise of Wisdom in chap. 24, he writes, "All these things are the book of the covenant of God Most High, The Law which Moses commanded" (v 23). In 33:2 he states that "he that hateth the law is not wise," and in 15:1 he says of Wisdom that "he that taketh hold of the Law *maketh* her *his companion.*"[57]

In this identification, Ben Sira has not given up the traditional sage orientation of Judaic wisdom, for the Torah is to be followed because it is sage, not sage advice because it is righteous. This point was made quite well in 1960 by Ernst Günter Bauckmann,[58] but it was questioned by Josef Haspecker,[59] who called attention to the importance of the theme of the fear of God in Ben Sira and who concluded that this, and therefore righteousness, was the primary interest of the book and that sagacity was subordinated to it. Such a position, however, is difficult to maintain in the face of what so many students of Ben Sira have called his "eudaemonism," and von Rad noted, against Haspecker, "that it is wisdom, and not, for example, the fear of God, that is the fundamental theme of" Ben Sira, which is affirmed "once again in the epilogue (50:27–29)."[60]

The way in which the identification is intended, however, has

---

[56] Cf. again the discussion of the fear of Yahweh, above, p. 4.

[57] Literally, "leads her in the path."

[58] Bauckmann, "Proverbien und Sprüche." Bauckmann cited, along with numerous other texts, Sir 32:24: "He that observeth the Law guardeth himself, And he that trusteth in Yahweh shall not be brought to shame," and he concluded that "whoever decides for God decides at the same time for the continuation of his life, health, wealth, honor, and strength" (Bauckmann, "Proverbien und Sprüche," 51).

[59] Haspecker, *Gottesfurcht*. Crenshaw, *Wisdom*, 153–54, endorses Haspecker's view. Yet Crenshaw also, *Wisdom*, 167, n, 11, correctly observes that "Sirach supplements human inquiry with divine revelation. The Torah thus becomes material with which the sages work in their attempts to master reality."

[60] Von Rad, *Wisdom in Israel*, 242.

continued to attract scholarly interest, and E. P. Sanders has proposed, more recently, that "the relationship is dialectical, and neither subordinates the other," since "the universal quest for wisdom . . . is really answered in the Mosaic covenant."[61] It seems to me, however, that, while Ben Sira may make *statements* in which Torah and wisdom are identified on an equal basis (E. P. Sanders's dialectic), the *content* of his advice is overwhelmingly sage and not legal.[62] In other words, Ben Sira may make statements to the effect that "the universal quest for wisdom . . . is really answered in the Mosaic covenant," as he does in 24:23 when he says that "all these things are the book of the covenant of God Most High, The Law which Moses commanded"; the actual content of his advice, however, is sage and is related to the practical goal of the preservation of one's good name. Thus in the important "doubled decalogue about shame" in 41:16–42:8 he includes, along with an emphasis on the Torah (42:2), such advice as that one should not stretch out one's elbow at a meal (41:19) or that one should not repeat a rumor (42:1ab). Ben Sira apparently *thought* that the best way to achieve the goal of a "truly shamefast" life (42:1cd) was to follow the Torah, yet he drew most of the details of his *advice* on how to achieve it not from the Torah, but from sage traditions and observation. We now turn to another aspect of this issue.

One of the most pronounced aspects in Ben Sira is the concern for one's good name and the attendant caution that informs his ethical advice.[63] "Doth a noble draw near? keep at a distance," he advises in 13:9, and he continues (vv 9–11):

> And so much the more will he cause thee to approach.
> Do not thyself draw near, lest thou be put at a distance;
> And keep not (too) far away, lest *thou be hated*.
> Venture not to be free with him,
> And mistrust his much conversation.
> For *in his much conversation there are tests*,
> And when he smileth at thee he is probing thee.

The need for caution extends through all of life's relationships, as is clear from 6:13, "Separate thyself from thine enemies, And be on thy guard against thy friends"; and it applies also to the practice of righteousness,

---

[61] E. P. Sanders, *Paul and Palestinian Judaism. A Comparison of Patterns of Religion* (Philadelphia: Fortress, 1977) 332.

[62] J. Hadot, *Penchant mauvais et volonté libre dans la Sagesse de Ben Sira.* (Bruxelles: Presses Universitaires, 1970) 83, compares Ben Sira's use of the word Torah to that of the author of (wisdom) Psalm 119. Ryssel, "Jesus Sirach," 230–31, also sees the sage interest as dominant.

[63] For a more detailed discussion of this point, cf. my article, "Ben Sira's Ethics of Caution."

as in 29:20: "Help thy neighbor according to thy power, And take heed to thyself that thou fall not." Caution and righteousness are even equated by juxtaposing different meanings of the verb *šmr*, as in "to guard oneself" and "to keep the commandment"; thus 32:23: "In all thy works guard thyself, For he that so doeth keepeth the commandment." It is in 41:12–13, however—at the climax of the body of Ben Sira's work just preceding the praise of the god of nature—that one sees the supreme importance of a good name and the caution that must protect it. Here Ben Sira admonishes, "Be in fear for thy name, for that abideth longer for thee Than thousands of treasures *of wisdom. The value of* a life lasts for *a number of* days, But the *value* of a name for days without number."[64]

The importance of the name is paramount. Of the Fathers he is about to praise at such great length he affirms in 44:14 that "their bodies were buried in peace, But their name liveth unto all generations"; and in an earlier proverb he had also stated the same principle in more general terms: "Who is wise (for his) people gaineth honour, And his name abideth in life eternal" (37:26). This importance of the name is mentioned frequently in Ben Sira, as for example in 5:15–16: "Deal not corruptly either in a small or a great matter; And be not an enemy in place of a friend, (For then) wouldst thou *inherit* an evil name, and *dishonour*, and reproach." In order for one to be properly cautious regarding one's name, of course, it is necessary to have a proper sense of shame, and so Ben Sira follows his climactic statement about the importance of the name in 41:11–13 with the "doubled decalogue about shame," 41:16–42:8, in which he advises both caution ("Be ashamed . . . Of a master and a mistress of deceit, Of an assembly and a people of transgression, Of a comrade and friend of treachery," 41:18) and proper righteousness ("Of these things be not ashamed, . . . Of the Law of the Most High, and the statute; And of justice, to do right by the wicked," 42:2). Thus one may also note 32:24: "He that observeth the Law guardeth himself, And he that trusteth in Yahweh shall not be brought to shame." Shame as sanction both for righteousness and for caution is again seen in 4:20–28, where Ben Sira advises (v 21) that "there is a shame that is the *portion* of iniquity, And there is a shame (that *is the portion of*) honour and favor"; so that we may note that it is in his discussion of shame that Ben Sira most emphatically equates sage caution and Torah righteousness.

While occasional reference can be found in the Book of Proverbs to the importance of a good name and of the proper shame that supports and protects the name, this does not become a theme of any particular

---

[64] Ben Sira may well have been reformulating here Prov 22:1, "A [good] name is to be chosen rather than great riches" (so Middendorp, *Stellung*, 81); yet the emphasis he places on the name in his work goes far beyond what one finds in Proverbs.

importance in Proverbs. One may note, for example, Prov 22:1: "A name
is to be chosen rather than great riches, and favor is better than silver or
gold";[65] or 10:5: "A son who gathers in summer is prudent, but a son
who sleeps in harvest brings shame." Yet life is in the Book of Proverbs
the primary motivation for sage or proper behavior, and life in fact
stands in the earlier proverbial tradition in the same place in which the
good name stands for Ben Sira, as the theme around which sage caution
and proper righteousness tend to coalesce.[66] One sees this principle at
work in Prov 4:4 and 7:2: "Keep my commandments, and live"; in 10:17:
"*The path of life is the keeping of training*"; in 13:14: "The teaching of
the wise *man* is a fountain of life"; and in the variant of the last, 14:27:
"The fear of Yahweh is a fountain of life."

In this and the other characteristics of Ben Sira identified to this point
as being different from those of the Book of Proverbs—except for the
naming of the author—the differences are not absolute but relative:
Certain tendencies may be seen to be already at work which then reach a
fuller development in Ben Sira. Yet such an explanation of differences is
never entirely adequate, for it fails to explain why tendencies move in
certain directions. Or, observed from another perspective, what appear as
tendencies are seen to be such only when the several documents in which
the observed differences occur are seen in a developmental relationship
with one another. If one read, for example, only the Book of Proverbs, one
would not discover a "tendency" toward the increasing importance of one's
name and the attendant shame and toward the decreasing importance of
life as ethical motivation. One would discover rather that life is very
important in the Book of Proverbs and that a name and shame are of minor
importance. It is only when Ben Sira is brought into the picture that one
might suggest that a tendency is at work; but another way to describe the
relationship of Ben Sira to the earlier proverbial tradition in this respect is
to affirm that Ben Sira is different from the earlier proverbial tradition,
although not absolutely so. It will be possible in the pages that follow to
attempt a partial explanation of these differences, but it is necessary for the
moment simply to note them clearly.

Divergencies in Specific Details

A number of more specific details in Ben Sira may also be
distinguished from the earlier proverbial tradition. Probably the most
obvious of these are the long praise of the god of nature in 42:15–43:33
and the extended Praise of the Fathers in 44:1–50:24, for which

---

[65] Cf. also Qoh 7:1.
[66] Cf. also Crenshaw, *Wisdom*, 62. Crenshaw further, p. 153, has not noted the shift in
Ben Sira from life to shame.

precedents hardly exist in the Judaic proverbial tradition.[67] These major sections of Ben Sira are generally recognized as unique individual traits of the work, although there are antecedents to the praise of the god of nature especially in Job, and also in the Psalter, e.g., Psalm 19.[68] Another unique portion of Ben Sira's advice is his encouragement of proper dining and banqueting habits in 31:12–32:13. Prov 23:1–3 had advised:

> When you sit down to eat with a ruler,
>> observe carefully what is before you;
> and put a knife to your throat
>> if you are a man given to appetite.
> Do not desire his delicacies,
>> for they are deceptive food;

and to this may be compared Sir 31:12, 14, and 16b:

> *My son*, if thou sittest at a great man's table,
>> Be not greedy upon it;

> Stretch not out the hand wherever he may look,
>> And collide not with him in the dish.[69]

> Eat like a man what is put before thee,
>> And be not *gluttonous*, lest thou be *rejected*.

Ben Sira, however, goes quite beyond this advice of normal banquetary obsequiousness to advise general caution at the table (31:15), proper order in eating (31:17–18), moderation in eating (31:19–20) and the ancient version of seltzer (v 21), propriety in drinking (31:25–30), how to behave as a banquet master (32:1–2), and how to behave if elder (vv 3–6) or younger (vv 7–12). Such a total approach to banqueting mores appears to be unique to Ben Sira when regarded in terms of the extant Judaic wisdom tradition that precedes him.

A proper concern for the dead is also something new in Ben Sira within the Judaic proverbial wisdom tradition. "My son, let tears fall over the dead; Show thy grief," he advises, "and wail out thy lamentation. In accordance with what is due to him bury his body, And hide not thyself when he expires" (38:16). Similarly also his description in 28:13–26 of the evil wrought by the "third tongue." Here v 17, "The stroke of a whip maketh a mark, But the stroke of the tongue breaketh bones," is somewhat reminiscent of Prov 25:15, "A soft tongue will break a bone"; yet only the

---

[67] Smend, *Weisheit*, XXII, sees both sections as part of Ben Sira's attempt to represent a viable Judaism over against Hellenism; and Ryssel, "Jesus Sirach," 231, sees the two sections together as especially Judaic.

[68] A fuller discussion of the background and function of Sir 42:15–43:33 may be found below, pp. 75–80.

[69] Reading *tyḥd* with Bmg. for *dyḥd*.

figure is the same, for the two proverbs have opposite meanings, since the Book of Proverbs speaks of persuasion, Ben Sira of mischief.[70] Sir 28:18, which refers to those who "have fallen through the tongue," might also call to mind Prov 17:20, "one with a perverse tongue falls into calamity." The term, "third tongue," however, does not occur in the proverbial tradition prior to Ben Sira, and the Book of Proverbs, when it speaks of the tongue *in malam partem*, refers to the "lying (*šāqer*)" or "perverse (*tahpukâ*)" tongue, as in 17:20 or 10:31. Most of the section in Ben Sira, however, is unparalleled in the tradition, e.g., 28:14–15:

> The third tongue hath *shaken many*,
>   And hath dispersed them among many nations;
> Even strong cities hath it *pulled down*,
>   And *overturned* the dwellings of the great.
> The third tongue hath cast out brave women,
>   And deprived them of their labours.

Finally one should note, among those traits which distinguish Ben Sira from the earlier proverbial tradition, his praise of the profession of the sage, 38:24–39:11. Here he affirms that "the wisdom of the scribe *cometh by opportunity of leisure*,[71] And he that hath little business can become wise" (38:24); and, in 39:1–11 (partially quoted above),[72] he extols the learned sage, whose

> . . . memory shall not cease,
>   And his name shall live from generation to generation.
> His wisdom *do* the *nations* tell forth,
>   And his praise the assembly publisheth.
> If he live long, he shall *leave a name* more than a thousand;
>   And when he cometh to an end, *it* sufficeth *for him*.

There can be little doubt that the fairly large body of material in Ben Sira that has little or no relation to the proverbs, themes, or organizational principles of the Book of Proverbs is to be explained in part as Ben Sira's unique contribution to the proverbial wisdom tradition. Surely his observations of the world about him are reflected in his book! Yet Ben Sira's originality may lie more in the nature of his selective and organizational process than in his original formulation of totally new proverbs; for, as he himself informs us, the ideal sage is one

> Who searcheth out the wisdom of all the ancients,
>
> Who serveth among great men,

---

[70] I assume that Ben Sira quotes the Book of Proverbs here and shifts its meaning.

[71] The parallelism of the verse dictates that the Greek, *en eukairiq scholēs*, is to be preferred as representing the more likely original reading over the Hebrew, *trbh ḥkmh*.

[72] Cf. p. 12.

And appeareth before princes;
Who travelleth through the lands of *other* peoples,
Testeth good and evil among men. (39:1, 4)

Such a statement raises the possibility that much of the "non-proverbial"
material in Ben Sira is the result of the influence upon him of other traditions. What other identifiable influences have played into Ben Sira's
compendium of advice and wisdom? While it is our primary purpose in
this volume to investigate the possibility of influence from Egyptian
wisdom of the Ptolemaic period, some account must first be given of
other discernible traditions in Ben Sira.

Non-Proverbial Wisdom

The first and most obvious is the one that has been mentioned
already several times in passing in the course of the discussion of Ben
Sira's relation to the Book of Proverbs—that is the unconventional
wisdom books, Job and Qoheleth, as well as the Psalms. Gordis, in his
commentary on Qoheleth, has indicated several instances of Ben Sira's
reliance on Qoheleth, and we may conveniently note them here.[73] (The
parallels already cited need not, I trust, be repeated.)

The theme of another's reaping the benefits of one's toil, expressed in
Qoh 4:8 and 6:2, "For whom am I toiling and depriving myself of pleasure? . . . a man to whom God gives wealth, possessions, and honor, . . .
but a stranger enjoys them," seems to be repeated in Sir 14:4: "He that
withholdeth from himself gathereth for another, And a stranger shall
satiate himself with his goods." Similarly, Qoheleth's words in Qoh 7:14,
"In the day of prosperity be joyful, and in the day of adversity consider;
God has made the one as well as the other," seem to find an echo in Sir
33:14–15: "Over against evil (stands) the good, and against death life;
Likewise over against the godly the sinner. Even thus look upon all the
works of God, Each different, one the opposite of the other." The
language of Qoh 3:11, "He has made everything beautiful in its time,"
also seems to have influenced Sir 39:16: "[The works of] God are all good,
And he supplies every need in its season." One of the most obvious
parallels is readily seen only in Hebrew: Qoh 3:15, *hā'elōhîm yĕbaqqēš
et-nirdāp*, and Sir 5:3, *yy' mbqš nrdpym*. (Gordis renders Qoh 3:15 as
"God always seeks to repeat the past"; Ben Sira apparently intends
something similar, but his meaning is more obscure.) Similarly, the
comparable phrases *'dm pnyw yšn'* . . . (Qoh 8:1) and *'nwš yšn' pnyw*
(Sir 13:24) may be noted; and Qoheleth's advice in 7:16, "Do not make
yourself overwise; why should you destroy yourself?" seems to have been
revised slightly in Sir 32:4: "At an unseasonable time *why will you be*

73 Gordis, *Koheleth*, 46–48.

wise?" Further, Ben Sira's advice in 26:19,

> My son, keep thyself healthy in the flower of thine age,
>   And give not thy strength unto strangers.
> Having found a portion of good soil out of all the land,
>   Sow it with thine own seed . . . ,

may reflect the language (although not the meaning) of Qoh 11:6, 9: "In the morning sow your seed. . . . Rejoice, O young man, in your youth." Finally, one may note Qoh 8:5, "He who obeys a command will meet no harm," and Sir 15:15, "If thou (so) desirest, thou canst keep the commandment, *And if thou trust in him, of a truth thou shalt live.*"[74]

The primary connections between Ben Sira and the Book of Job are found in the self-praise of Wisdom in Ben Sira 24 and in the long praise of the god of nature in Sir 39:12–35; 42:15–43:33. These two sections receive extensive discussion below, the one in chap. 2 and the other in chap. 3, where the connections with Job are noted, and perhaps it will be sufficient here simply to refer to those discussions.

Ben Sira likely thought of the Psalter as a didactic wisdom book, and its influence is also to be found in his work, although it hardly represents a major strand.[75] Thus Ps 33:3, "Sing to him a new song, play skillfully on the strings, with loud shouts," probably is echoed in Sir 39:15: "With songs of harp and *all kinds of music*; And thus shall ye say, with a shout"; and Ps 68:5, which praises God as "Father of the fatherless and protector of widows," seems to be taken over by Ben Sira in 4:10 as advice: "Be as a father to orphans, And in place of a husband to widows." Ps 107:23–24 explains that

> Some went down to the sea in ships,
>   doing business on the great waters;
> they saw the deeds of Yahweh,
>   his wondrous works in the deep;

and this phrasing seems to be taken up by Ben Sira in his praise of the

---

[74] A few other parallels listed by Gordis are not included here, simply in the interest of economy. A slightly different list is given by R. Kroeber, *Der Prediger, hebräisch und deutsch* (Schriften und Quellen der alten Welt 13; Berlin: Akademie-Verlag, 1963) 65–66. C. F. Whitley, *Koheleth. His Language and Thought* (BZAW 148; Berlin and New York: de Gruyter, 1979) 122–31, has argued that the parallels between Qoheleth and Ben Sira should be read as showing a dependence, if at all, in the other direction. While that relationship between the two works seems less likely to me, it is not a matter of great significance here, since the purpose of this chapter is solely to point out what everyone already knows: that Ben Sira relies heavily on Judaic tradition. In the chapters following it will be better to err on the side of caution and to assume that, if parallels to Ben Sira appear both in Qoheleth and in some foreign literature, we should conclude that the foreign parallel has *not* provided the theme or statement in question to Ben Sira.

[75] The following parallels are taken from Middendorp, *Stellung*, 72–75.

god of nature, 43:24–25:

> They that go down to the sea tell of its extent,
>   And when our ears hear it we are astonished.
> Therein are marvels, the most wondrous of His works,
>   All kinds of living things, and the monsters in *great number.*

Sir 11:1, again, "The wisdom of the poor man lifteth up his head, And causeth him to sit among princes," appears to predicate of Wisdom what Ps 113:7–8 says of God:

> He raises the poor from the dust,
>   and lifts the needy from the ash heap,
> to make them sit with princes,
>   with the princes of his people.

Finally, there is a possible reliance of Sir 43:17–20 on Ps 147:18, since both refer to God's power as demonstrated in snow, hoar-frost, and ice, in that order, although Ben Sira's description is considerably more elaborate.

Thus we see that Ben Sira was quite aware of the unconventional wisdom books and that he has quoted from them or, perhaps better, employed their language. It should also be noted, however, that they do not represent a significant *influence.* Only in the matter of the organization of the book is there any possibility that the unconventional wisdom books are responsible for or explain the presence of the "non-proverbial remainder" of Ben Sira; and even there one may reasonably doubt that Ben Sira organized his book in the way that he did because he had read Qoheleth. More likely we see in Ben Sira a later stage of a trend already present in Qoheleth and in Proverbs 1–9. It is otherwise, however, with the next element of Judaic tradition to be discussed.[76]

The Torah

Probably the most obvious "new" element in Ben Sira is another Judaic strand, but one that is of too late currency to have influenced much of the earlier proverbial tradition. That element is, of course, the Deuteronomic Torah.[77] Oesterley wrote, "Ben-Sira gives great prominence to the Law both in its ethical and ritual aspects, differing in this markedly from Proverbs . . . ; and the stress which he lays on the importance of the Law, and legal observances generally, marks his book out as perhaps the most

---

[76] It can also be readily demonstrated, of course, that Ben Sira made use of material in both the Former and the Latter Prophets, as well as in the other books of the Writings. Indeed, as his grandson wrote, Ben Sira gave "himself much to the reading of the Law and the Prophets and the other books of the fathers." It is beyond the purposes of this volume to discuss his use of those works further, but such use does need to be noted.

[77] Crenshaw, *Wisdom*, 150, refers to "the powerful influence of Yahwism" on Ben Sira; cf. further ibid., 150–53.

striking link we have between the older and the newer Judaism."[78] When
even the later authors of the Book of Proverbs used the words *tôrâ* and
miṣwâ, they meant the instruction and counsel of the sage. Thus Prov 7:2:
"Keep my commandments (*miṣwōtay*) and live, keep my *teaching*
(*tôrātîy*) as the apple of your eye." In Ben Sira, however, these terms apply
to the (Deuteronomic) Torah. In 39:1 he gives, as the *first* characteristic of
the ideal sage, that he "applieth himself" and that he "*setteth* his mind
upon the Law of the Most High"; and, in 42:2, he lists *first* in his catalog of
things of which one should not be ashamed "the Law of the Most High, and
the statute; And of justice, to do right by the wicked." "Fear of God (*dḥl
l'lh'* = *yārē' 'ĕlōhîm*)"[79] and "statute (*ḥôq*)" are emphatically Deuteronomic terms (cf. Deut 6:2 *et passim*). His repeated association of Wisdom with
the fear of Yahweh in 1:11–20 (cited above, p. 4) further likely betrays this
orientation, as does his statement in 1:26, "If thou desire Wisdom, keep the
commandments (*entolai* = *miṣwôt*), And the Lord will give her freely unto
thee"; and the somewhat different association in chap. 24 again shows his
basic allegiance to the Torah. This allegiance can be seen in the way in
which he identifies wisdom and Torah in 24:8: "The Creator of all things
gave me commandment, And He that created me fixed my dwelling-place
(for me); And He said: Let thy dwelling-place be in Jacob, And in Israel
take up thine inheritance"; or in his affirmation about wisdom-Torah in vv
23, 25: "All these things are the book of the covenant of God Most High,
The Law which Moses commanded *us* (as) an heritage for the assemblies of
Jacob, Which filleth (men) with wisdom. . . ." Ben Sira's emphasis on the
fear of Yahweh even led Josef Haspecker to conclude that the fear of
Yahweh was *the* primary theological theme in the work.[80]

It is further possible that Deuteronomic language has influenced Ben
Sira's language of caution, since the way in which Ben Sira equates sage
caution with the keeping of the Law—

> In all thy paths guard thyself (*šĕmôr napšĕkā*),
>   For everyone that so doeth keepeth the commandment
>   (*šômēr miṣwâ*).
> In all thy works guard thyself,
>   For he that so doeth keepeth the commandment
>
>   (Sir 32:23)

—may rely on Deut 4:9, "only take heed (*hiššāmer lĕkā*), and keep your
self (*šĕmōr napšĕkā*) diligently, lest you forget the things which your eyes

---

[78] Oesterley, *APOT* 1.304. To the degree that Oesterley meant that Ben Sira marked a
transition from the "good" Old Testament to the "bad" (legalistic) Judaism, his sentiment
is to be rejected as unsound; cf. E. P. Sanders, *Paul*.

[79] The parallelism dictates accepting the Syriac over the Greek as the more likely
original. So also Box and Oesterley.

[80] Above, pp. 15–16.

have seen."[81] The continuing success of Deuteronomy is seen, therefore, not only in Ben Sira's allegiance to the Torah, but in his identification of Torah with wisdom and in his carrying over into the heart of his sage advice terms and concepts which have a Deuteronomic origin.

The preceding discussion has been presented not as a demonstration, but rather only as a reminder, at most as a clarification, of the obvious— Ben Sira's use of Judaic tradition. Perhaps nothing is clearer about his book than that he stands squarely within Judaic tradition: first of all the proverbial sapiential tradition of the Book of Proverbs, then the tradition of Torah righteousness, and finally the entire body of Judaic wisdom. One need refer, apart from the evidence itself, only to such standard discussions of Ben Sira as T. A. Burkill's article on Ben Sira in the *Interpreter's Dictionary of the Bible* or James Crenshaw's recent introduction to the wisdom books to observe the near universal agreement on this point.[82] While the remainder of this study will deal with Ben Sira's use and adaptation of foreign works and traditions, it will still be everywhere obvious that the roots of his thought lie primarily in his Judaic traditions. But we have also noted that Ben Sira departs from known Judaic tradition at certain sometimes significant points. The inquiry that follows may be understood as an attempt to discover whether and to what degree what is new in Ben Sira—when his work is compared with earlier Judaic tradition—can be explained as the result of his having appropriated non-Judaic sources for his thought.

---

[81] So H. Duesberg and P. Auvray, *Le Livre de l'Ecclésiastique* (La Sainte Bible; Paris: Editions du Cerf, 1958) 149; Smend, *Weisheit*, 295; Box and Oesterley.

[82] T. A. Burkill, "Ecclesiasticus," *IDB* 2, 13–21 and Crenshaw, *Wisdom*, 149–73, 256–57.

CHAPTER 2

BEN SIRA'S RELATION TO HELLENIC TRADITION

Preliminary Observations

The discussion of the continuity and discontinuity between Ben Sira and the Jewish wisdom tradition, and of the way in which the influence of Deuteronomy and the Torah help to explain the discontinuity, prepares us for the logical next step of the inquiry, an analysis of Hellenistic, specifically Hellenic influence on Ben Sira's thinking. For any writer within the Greek sphere of influence during the Hellenistic period such influence may be assumed before it is proved, so that, regarding Jewish writers of this period, Moses Hadas has even written that "every work in the Apocrypha and Pseudepigrapha of the Old Testament has expressions from or allusions to tragedy which the reader was obviously expected to recognize."[1] One may thus expect to find such "expressions and allusions" in Ben Sira; but two distinctions must be clearly noted at the outset of this inquiry. The first is that between use of the *work* of another author and use of a *phrase* which may have become so current that it was simply part of the stock of "expressions and allusions" available to everyone. If, for example, Ben Sira uses language reminiscent of the *Iliad* or of the *Odyssey* in a half dozen or so places (and we shall see that there is only one clear use of a few lines from the *Iliad*), should we conclude that he had read the *Iliad* and found it useful, or would we be safe only in asserting that he had used one or a few phrases in common parlance, the ultimate origin of which is known to those of us who have read the *Iliad*? A modern equivalent would be the use of Shakespearean language. While Shakespeare is probably less read by educated people today in the western world than Homer was in Ben Sira's day in the Hellenistic world, many of Shakespeare's phrases have entered the common parlance of the language. If a writer should write that "all that glitters is not gold" or that "we're all players on a stage"[2] but should use

[1] Hadas, *Hellenistic Culture*, 130.

[2] The misquotations of Shakespeare are intended and are given here in forms in which I have often heard them. I have in this way attempted to render "expressions and allusions" to Shakespeare in English that are analogous to the "expressions from and allusions to" Hellenic literature in Ben Sira which have been seen by various authors and

no other apparently Shakespearean language, we should probably be more correct in concluding that the writer merely used a couple of current phrases than in assuming that he had read Shakespeare and had found that author instructive.[3]

The other distinction that we must make is that between the taking over of a Hellenic concept such as, say, the Golden Mean or pride in physical accomplishment and the mere use of convenient language (whether a deliberate citation or not) to express a Judaic idea. Sometimes it might be impossible to do the one without doing the other; for example, if Ben Sira had cited the Delphic maxim, *mēden agan*, "nothing overmuch," he would of necessity have endorsed the concept of moderation. The use of many figures of speech from Greek literature, however, would be possible without thereby bringing over any specifically Greek concept. In the following discussion, we shall be interested in evidence for all the possibilities just distinguished, since we want to see how Hellenic culture influenced Ben Sira, but we shall be especially concerned to determine the degree to which Greek thinking has influenced the thinking of our Hellenistic Jewish sage.

Several authors have endeavored to show parallels between Ben Sira and Greek literature, and the names of Bigot, Treves, and Glasson deserve especially to be mentioned.[4] Th. Middendorp, more recently,[5] has gone over and distilled the evidence presented by these and other authors, and we may conveniently follow his presentation of the evidence.

Middendorp cites, by his count, "about one hundred" places in Ben Sira for which, in his opinion, convincing parallels in Greek literature can be found.[6] There are by my count 163 separate passages in Greek literature listed by Middendorp as similar to or the source of these approximately one hundred passages in Ben Sira, and they present a noteworthy variety. Sixty-two or 38 percent of all the Greek parallels given are from Theognis. Euripides is a distant second with nineteen, but no more than three are from any one play (Middendorp gives parallels from eleven plays of Euripides and from the collection of *fragmenta incerta*). Citations from Xenophon are the next most numerous (thirteen); there are eleven from Hesiod (ten from the *Works and Days*), three from the *Iliad*

to an examination of which we are proceeding. Also with Ben Sira, we almost nowhere deal with literal and direct quotations of any Greek writer, but generally only with "expressions and allusions" which may have originated somewhere in Hellenic literature.

[3] Gordis, *Koheleth*, 56, makes the same point about Qoheleth by referring to the modern use of such terms as "class struggle" by persons who have never read Marx, and other similar examples.

[4] L. Bigot, "Livre de l'Ecclésiastique," *DTC* 4/2 (1920) cols. 2025–54; M. Treves, *Studi su Gesù ben Sirach* (Estratto da la Rassegna Mensile di Israel 22/9–10; Città di castello, 1956); T. F. Glasson, *Greek Influence in Jewish Eschatology* (London: S.P.C.K., 1961).

[5] Middendorp, *Stellung*.

[6] Ibid., 24. The parallels are presented on pp. 8–24.

and five from the *Odyssey*, seven from Sophocles, and from one to five from each of a number of other Greek authors, great and small. Middendorp draws one obvious conclusion from this evidence: Ben Sira had read the elegiac poems of Theognis[7] but had probably used a chrestomathy for his other Greek material.[8] Before undertaking to examine Middendorp's evidence in some detail, we must note a peculiarity about Ben Sira's presumed use of Greek material to which Middendorp draws attention. It is that the Greek "expressions and allusions," to use Hadas's language again, are invariably similar to what is in the Bible, i.e., to what is in the Law, the Prophets, and the earlier wisdom books, especially the Book of Proverbs. Middendorp's explanation of this phenomenon is that Ben Sira deliberately chose sayings from Greek authors that resembled the Jewish proverbial tradition in order to show his Jewish readers the value of Gentile wisdom[9] and to show his "Hellenic educated reader[s]" (does he mean Gentiles?) "the great similarities between Hellenistic and Jewish thought."[10] Aside from the fact that an intended Gentile readership for Ben Sira is hardly to be assumed, Middendorp's explanation of Ben Sira's use of Hellenic literature severely undercuts attempts to prove the existence of meaningful parallels between Ben Sira and Hellenic literature. We know that Ben Sira read the Bible (i.e., the Law, the Prophets, and what his grandson calls "the others"); we do not know in advance what else he may have read. When, therefore, a line in Ben Sira might be a paraphrase or a restating of something in the Bible, the evidence must be remarkably strong in order to make a convincing argument that Ben Sira has relied at that point on some line from Hellenic literature. Furthermore, as we saw above in the examples of parallels between Ben Sira and the Book of Proverbs, Ben Sira almost never quotes exactly. His work is his own, however much he relies on the proverbial tradition, and his reliance on his traditions is not merely the work of a tradent. Thus, when we see that what has gone into the blender of his thinking comes from Jewish tradition, we also see that what comes out is also the product of Ben Sira's own religious and ideological persuasion (one may recall his caution/shame ethics, for example). With this point clarified, we may turn to a partial examination of Middendorp's evidence for Hellenic parallels.

Theognis

It would appear that Ben Sira did, indeed, read and use the elegiac poems of Theognis, at least Book 1 (Book 2 is bawdy and could hardly

---

[7] Ibid., 13, 25.
[8] Ibid., 25.
[9] Ibid., 8, 25.
[10] Ibid., 84; cf. also p. 25.

have been appreciated by so religious a person as Ben Sira). These poems were quite famous and were mentioned by both Plato and Aristotle, and Xenophon even wrote a treatise, *On Theognis*.[11] This fame, the fact that Theognis's work is primarily practical advice much like that of the Jewish sages, and the further fact that the elegiac couplet employed by Theognis quite resembles Hebrew poetry with its *parallelismus membrorum* might all have recommended the work to Ben Sira. That Ben Sira did find Theognis useful may be seen, for example, in the parallels between certain lines of Theognis and Sir 6:5–17, the section on true and false friends.

We saw above (p. 7) that this section of Ben Sira appears to continue the sentiment of Prov 18:24, "There are friends who pretend to be friends, but there is a friend who sticks closer than a brother." This theme is hardly carried out further in Proverbs, however (cf. Prov 19:4, 7), and some lines of Theognis are strikingly close to Sir 6:5–17. Theog. 115–16 says that "many, for sure, are cup-and-trencher friends, but few a man's comrades in a grave matter,"[12] which is quite similar to Sir 6:10: "There is a friend who is a table-friend, But he is not to be found in the day of affliction."[13] Still closer to this line of Ben Sira, however, is the doublet in Theognis of 115–116—643–44: "Many become comrades dear beside the bowl, but few in a grave matter,"[14] where the *polloi . . . krētēri philoi ginontai hetairoi* of Theog. 643 corresponds almost exactly to Ben Sira's language: *yš 'whb ḥbr šlḥn*.[15] The next verse of Ben Sira (6:11) observes that "when thou art in prosperity he will be like thee, *And when thou are in adversity he will depart from thee*," which is again similar to Theog. 697–98: "When I am in good plight my friends are many; if aught ill befall, there's but few whose hearts are true."[16] Further, Theognis's statement of the opening condition, *eu . . . echontos emou*, is again virtually the same as Ben Sira's *bṭwbtk*. The theme is frequent in Theognis. Thus Theog. 81–82 observes that there are few who would "suffer . . . in thy good fortune and thy bad"; and 299 says that "nobody's lief to be a man's friend when evil befals [*sic*] him" (in which Theognis's *kakon* is of course comparable to Ben Sira's *r‘h*.[17] Theog. 929–30, finally, explains that, "if thou be rich, thy friends are

[11] Cf. the evidence for the fame of Theognis in *Elegy and Iambus . . . with the Anacreontea* 1 (LCL; ed. and trans. J. M. Edmonds; Cambridge, Mass.: Harvard Univ. Press, 1968) 216–28.

[12] This and all translations from Theognis are from the work cited in the preceding note.

[13] Middendorp, *Stellung*, 15.

[14] Middendorp, ibid.

[15] In Theog. 115 simply *eisin hetairoi*.

[16] Middendorp, *Stellung*, 15. So also the following parallels to this verse.

[17] Translated "adversity" above after Box and Oesterley's translation of the rejected Hebrew stich (*APOT* 1).

many, and if poor, they are few."

The second stich of the Hebrew line of Sir 6:11, it should be noted, was rejected by Box and Oesterley in favor of the Greek, "And will lord it over thy servants." They argued, quite reasonably, that the proper antithesis did not come until v 12, and that the presumed original second stich represented by the Greek continued the meaning of the thesis, i.e., that the fair weather friend would behave as did the one to whom he was befriended.[18] The evidence from Theognis, however—especially lines 697–98 and 929–30—may support the originality of the Hebrew text of Ben Sira at this point.

Middendorp finds a parallel to Sir 6:13, "Separate thyself from thine enemies, And be on thy guard against thy friends," in Theog. 575, "My friends it is that betray me; for mine enemy can I shun."[19] The aptness of this parallel can be seen further in the fact that here Ben Sira's statement about the enemy, *mšn'yk hbdl*, is again virtually an exact rendering of Theognis's Greek, *ton g' echthron aleumai*. For Sir 6:15, "A faithful friend is beyond price, And his worth cannot be weighed," Middendorp lists as parallel Theog. 77–78: "In a sore dissension, Cyrnus, a trusty man is to be reckoned against gold and silver,"[20] where, in addition to the theme of friendship contrasted favorably to monetary value, the phrase *'whb 'mwnh* may be noted as comparable to Theognis's *pistos anēr*. It thus appears that Ben Sira made use of the maxims of Theognis in his detailing of the theme of true and false friendship, a theme which he has inherited from the Jewish proverbial tradition, but for his elaboration of which he does not mind relying on a Greek writer who had had some worthwhile (in Ben Sira's opinion) thoughts on the matter.

Other apparent reliance on Theognis may be noted. Middendorp cites, again on the theme of friendship, Sir 9:10a, "Foresake not an old friend, For the new is not . . . ," and Theog. 1151–52, "Never be thou persuaded by the words of men of the baser sort to leave the friend thou hast and seek another," which is certainly close; and he also notes Sir 9:18, "A man (full) of tongue is *feared* in the city,[21] And he that is hasty in speech is detested," and Theog. 295–96, "To a talkative man silence is

---

[18] Box and Oesterley, *APOT* 1.335. So also Duesberg et Auvray, *Ecclésiastique*, 44; Smend, *Weisheit*, 55; C. Spicq, "L'Ecclésiastique," *La Saint Bible* (Paris: Letouzey et Ané, 1951), 599; A. Edersheim, "Ecclesiasticus," *The Holy Bible*, Apocrypha 2 (London: John Murray, 1888) 59. Not, however, Peters, *Jesus Sirach*, 57; or I. Lévi, *L'Ecclésiastique ou la Sagesse de Jésus, fils de Sira* 2 (Paris: Ernest Leroux, 1901) 32–33.

[19] Middendorp, *Stellung*, 15.

[20] Ibid.

[21] With Box and Oesterley, *APOT* 1, Duesberg et Auvray, *Ecclésiastique*, Smend, *Weisheit*, Spicq, "Ecclésiastique," Peters, *Jesus Sirach*, Lévi, *Ecclésiastique*, Edersheim, "Ecclesiasticus," I take the Greek to reflect the original *b'yr* instead of the text, *b'd*, which seems to make no sense—unless, of course, Theognis's "company" (*hoisi parē*) should lead us to read *b'dh*, "in the congregation."

a sore burden, and his speech a weariness to his company."[22] When we note further that line 297 of Theognis begins, "All hate him" (compare the *yšwn'* of Sir 9:18b), the possibility of Ben Sira's reliance on Theognis here is heightened.

We may next note Sir 10:6 and Theog. 323–26, where the reader is cautioned not to retaliate against a neighbor (Ben Sira) or friend (Theognis) for every wrong.[23] Here the language of Theog. 325, "If a man grow always angry (*epi panti cholǭto*) with a friend's offence (*hamartōl-ǭsi philōn*)," seems especially reminiscent of Sir 10:6a, "Requite not evil to thy neighbor (*'l tšlym r' lry'*) for *every* wrong (*[b]kl pš'*)." The similarity between Sir 12:3 and Theog. 105, further, is another case of parallelism cited by Middendorp,[24] and here we may note especially the similarity between Sir v 3a, *'yn twbh lmnwḥ rš'*, "there is no value in bestowing upon the wicked," and Theog. 108: . . . *oute kakous eu drōn eu palin antilabois*, "Thou wouldst [not] receive good again if thou didst good unto the bad."[25] There is also a possible connection between Sir 13:1, "Whoso toucheth pitch, it cleaveth to his hand, And he that associateth with a scorner will learn his way," and Theog. 35–36, "Of good men shalt thou learn good, but if thou mingle with the bad, thou shalt e'en lose the wit thou hast already."[26] If "learning a scorner's way" can be taken as comparable to "losing even the wit one has already," then the parallel is apt, for Ben Sira's *ḥwbr 'l lṣ* is roughly equivalent to Theognis's *kakoisin symmisgǭs*.

Middendorp may well be correct in comparing Sir 13:24 with Theog. 197,[27] for, while there are some noticeable differences (Theognis speaks of "A possession that cometh from Zeus [*Chrēma . . . Diothen*]," Ben Sira merely of "wealth [*'šyr*])," still Ben Sira's *'yn 'wn* "without sin," is another way of saying, as does Theognis, "of right (*syn dikǭ*)," and Ben Sira's beginning of the contrast in v 24b, *wr'*, is like the beginning of Theognis's contrast in line 200, *ei d'adikōs*.

There may be a connection between Theog. 1070A, B, "Be gay, my soul; there will be other men soon, but I shall be dead and become black earth," and Sir 14:16: ". . . indulge thy soul, For in Sheol there is no *seeking of* delight."[28] Now, there can be no doubt that Ben Sira is here

---

[22] Middendorp, *Stellung*, 16.

[23] Ibid. Prov 25:21–22 ("coals of fire") gives something of the same idea, but without any vocabulary connections, and then adds the theme of retribution.

[24] Middendorp, *Stellung*, 18.

[25] *Ps.-Phoc.* 152 is also similar: "Do no good to a bad man." P. W. Van der Horst, *The Sentences of Pseudo-Phocylides. With Introduction and Commentary* (SVTP 4; Leiden: Brill, 1978) 215, concludes that Pseudo-Phocylides was probably imitating Theog. 105–8.

[26] Middendorp, *Stellung*, 18.

[27] Ibid.

[28] Ibid., 19.

and in the immediately preceding verses repeating themes from Qoheleth. Especially in 14:11–19 he writes of the inevitableness of death and
of the need to enjoy the life at hand—one of Qoheleth's most pervasive
themes—and in 14:15 he refers again (cf. the earlier discussion of 14:4)[29]
to the misfortune of leaving one's wealth to another. For a comparable
expression in Qoheleth to Sir 14:16 one may refer to Qoh 9:9–10:[30]

> Enjoy life with the wife whom you love, all the days of your
> *ethereal* life which he has given you under the sun *all your ethe-*
> *real days*, because that is your portion in life and in your toil at
> which you toil under the sun. Whatever your hand finds to do, do
> it with your might; for there is no work or thought or knowledge
> or wisdom in Sheol, to which you are going.

Or one may note Qoh 11:8: "If a man lives many years, let him rejoice
in them all; but let him remember that the days of darkness will be
many"; and 12:7: "The dust returns to the earth as it was." Nevertheless,
one should bear in mind the following: Ben Sira's *pnq npšk*, while not
exactly the same as Theognis's *terpeo moi, phile thyme*, is still
reasonably close, and both are followed immediately in the same line
with the reference to black earth/Sheol. Furthermore, Ben Sira follows
this line closely (v 18) with an allusion to a passage from the *Iliad*
(discussed further below), which raises the possibility that we see him
here, as elsewhere, making use of Hellenic sayings that support his
Judaic position; but Theognis as source here remains uncertain.

Middendorp states flatly that Sir 27:22–23 is "obviously lifted from
Theognis," and he refers to Theog. 93–96.[31] The position is overstated,
since, while there is a similarity between v 23 and the lines in Theognis,
vv 22 and 24 seem to rely on Prov 6:12–19,[32] and, indeed, all three
verses in Ben Sira are likely motivated by that section of Proverbs.
Theognis wrote, "If one praise thee so long as he see thee, and speak ill
of thee behind thy back, such a comrade, for sure, is no very good
friend—the man, to wit, whose tongue speaks fair and his mind thinks
ill." The first part of this statement is rather like Ben Sira's v 23,

> Before thy face he speaketh sweetly,
>   And will admire thy words;
> But afterward he will alter his speech
>   And with thy words will make a stumbling-block;

---

[29] Above, p. 22.
[30] Cf. Kroeber, *Der Prediger*, 65.
[31] Middendorp, *Stellung*, 21.
[32] As Box and Oesterley, *APOT* 1, in their notes, imply. Cf. also Duesberg et Auvray,
Ecclésiastique, Smend, *Weisheit*, Ryssel, "Jesus Sirach," Edersheim, "Ecclesiasticus,"
Fritzsche, *Jesus-Sirach*.

and the second part of Theognis's statement would then make one think of Sir 27:22a, "He that winketh with his eye planneth evil things." Yet Prov 6:12–14 also refers to the "worthless person, a wicked man," who "winks with his eyes" and "with perverted heart devises evil" (ḥōrēš rā', apparently exactly the same as Ben Sira's "planneth evil things," so Segal); and Ben Sira's v 24, "Many things I hate, but nothing like him, And the Lord will hate him (too)," is surely "lifted" from Prov 6:16: "There are six things which Yahweh hates," following which are listed, among other "abominations," "a lying tongue" (v 17), "a heart that devises wicked plans" (v 18, language of v 14 and of Sir 27:22a again), "a false witness who breathes out lies, and a man who sows discord among brothers" (v 19). Thus it can be seen that there are several lines of connection between Sir 27:22–24 and Prov 6:12–19; nevertheless, Theognis's statement is more like Ben Sira's v 23 than is anything in Proverbs. It may well be the case, therefore, that we see here again a case of conflation on Ben Sira's part, whereby he has reworked a theme drawn from the Jewish proverbial tradition but has defined it further with the aid of a few lines from Theognis. While Middendorp does not raise this possibility in this particular instance, he does, as we have noted, generally observe this kind of conflation between Jewish and Hellenic material on Ben Sira's part, to which point we must return below.

In 30:17 Ben Sira writes, "Better death than an empty life, And eternal rest than continual pain," which is fairly close to Theog. 181–82: "To the needy, dear Cyrnus, death is better than a life oppressed with grievous Penury";[33] but Qoh 4:1–2 also notes that death is better than oppression.[34] A more likely connection is found when both Theognis and Ben Sira connect the refining qualities of fire on metal and of wine on men. Thus Theog. 499–500: "Cunning men know gold and silver in the fire; and the mind of a man . . . is shown by wine which he taketh"; and Sir 31:26: "A furnace proveth the work of the smith, So is wine in the quarrelling of the scornful."[35] Both Ben Sira and Theognis, furthermore, include considerable sections on the good and bad aspects of drinking (Theog. 467–510; Sir 31:24–31), for which not only the last but also the following parallels may be cited.

As parallels to Sir 31:28 Middendorp cites Theog. 211, 475, and 509–10.[36] Here as often his references are somewhat less than precise, but we may note that 211–12 is a doublet of 509–10, which reads, "The drinking of much wine is an ill; but if one drink it with knowledge, it is not an ill but a good"; and Sir 31:28–29 advises, "Joy of heart and

---

[33] Middendorp, Stellung, 22.
[34] On the other hand, Qoh 9:4 expresses the opposite viewpoint.
[35] Ibid., 23.
[36] Ibid.

gladness and delight Is wine drunk in season and (for) satisfaction. Head-ache, derision, and dishonour Is wine drunk in strife and vexation." Theog. 475, further, refers to the Hellenic measure (*metron*), a word which, it is worth noting, Ben Sira uses *only here in his entire work!*; v 27: "*As for the* water *of* wine, *it is life* to a man, If he drink it in moder-ation (*bmtkntw*)." To Sir 31:29-30, (v 29 above) "Much wine is for the fool a snare—It diminisheth strength and supplieth wounds," Midden-dorp cites as parallels from Theognis lines 413-14, 479-84, and 497-98. Lines 413-14 are not relevant here, since Theognis there affirms that he will not drink so much wine as to complain of his friend; but 497-98 both mentions the fool and notes the physical effects of drinking: "Wine maketh light the mind of wise and foolish alike, when they drink beyond their measure."[37] Lines 479-84, however, caution against shameful speech as a result of drinking, which is not Ben Sira's theme here. Finally, for this section, Middendorp cites Theog. 493-94 as parallel to Sir 31:31, "At a banquet of wine [*reproach* not] a friend, And *do not* . . ."[38] The parallel is again apt; Theog. 491-94: "He surely is invin-cible who shall say no vain thing when he hath drunken deep. But speak ye wisely albeit ye abide beside the bowl, withholding yourselves far from mutual strife." Here, also, Theog. 413-14 may be relevant: ". . . nor shall wine so far carry me away, as that I shall complain of thee."

In 41:3 Ben Sira writes, "Fear not Death, (it is) thy destiny," and Middendorp notes the closeness of Ben Sira's phrase, *mwt ḥwqyk*, to Theognis's *moira thanatou* in Theog. 819-20, "We have come into a much-desired mischief, Cyrnus, where best the fate of Death would take us both together."[39] While Theognis, however, may have influenced Ben Sira's language in this stich, the thought is apparently entirely biblical. Ben Sira continues in v 4, "This is the portion of all flesh from God, And how canst thou *reject* the *law* of the Most High!" Thus one must agree with Otto Kaiser that we have an "obvious allusion to Gen 3:19,"[40] "You

---

[37] Sir 31:29 is doubtless also to be related to Prov 23:29-30:

> Who has woe? Who has *pain*?
> Who has strife? Who has complaining?
> Who has wounds without cause?
> Who has *dullness* of eyes?
> Those who tarry long over wine,
> those who go to *seek* mixed wine;

cf. Middendorp, *Stellung*, 81.

[38] Ibid., 23.

[39] Ibid., 24.

[40] O. Kaiser, "Die Begründung der Sittlichkeit im Buche Jesus Sirach," *ZTK* 55 (1958) 57. Middendorp elsewhere (*Stellung*, 54) states that Sir 41:3-4 rests on Gen 6:13 and Job 20:29, and Box and Oesterley, *APOT* 1, also refer to Job 20:29. Gen 6:13 refers, however,

are dust, and to dust you shall return," and then note further that both
the sentiment and the use of the word "portion" are characteristic of
Qoheleth; cf. especially Qoh 9:2.[41]

All the parallels between Ben Sira and Theognis given by Middendorp that seem appropriate to me have now been discussed, and the
evidence seems to make it clear that Ben Sira did, in fact, read and use
Theognis. That is especially obvious in the sections on friendship and
drinking, where not only the general theme, but also similar formula-
tions and often strikingly similar language occur in both works; but there
are enough other close parallels to convince us that Ben Sira did not
limit his use of Theognis to those sections. Unfortunately, Ben Sira's use
of Theognis seems not to have been as extensive as indicated by Middendorp, since a number of the parallels he cites turn out, upon examination, to be inappropriate. A few of those may be mentioned here as
examples.

As a Theognis parallel to Sir 9:8ab, "Hide thine eye from a lovely
woman, And gaze not upon beauty which is not thine," Middendorp
cites Theog. 581, "I hate . . . a lustful man that chooseth to plough
another's land."[42] There is little connection here, however, since Ben Sira
is offering advice against the temptation provided by visual stimulation,
whereas Theognis merely opposes the adulterer. In any case, Ben Sira
surely relies here on Prov 6:20–7:5, where there is advice against various
kinds of sexual temptations and misconduct, as also in Sir 9:2–9; one may
note especially the mention of the "strange woman," the *zrh*, whose wiles
were so feared by the Jewish sages, in Prov 7:5 and Sir 9:3. Regarding
v 8, especially Prov 6:25–26 is relevant:

> Do not desire her beauty in your heart,
>   and do not let her capture you with her eyelashes;
> for a harlot may be hired for a loaf of bread,
>   but an adulteress stalks a man's very life.

Thus Sir 9:8c, further, provides the information that "by the comeliness
of a woman many have been ruined."

Sir 11:12 informs us that

> There is *one* that is weak and wandering in misery,
>   Lacking *everything* and abounding in frailty;
> And the eye of Yahweh watcheth him for good,
>   And He shaketh him up out of the stinking dust.

While Middendorp thinks that this verse is "reminiscent of Isa 52:2," he

---

to the destruction of all humanity in the flood, and Job 20:29 to the misfortune of the
wicked.

[41] Qoheleth does not refer, however, to death as one's portion.

[42] Middendorp, *Stellung*, 16.

nevertheless states that Theog. 485–90 "is similar in thought construction."[43] Now, in the first place, Isa 52:2 is similar to Sir 11:12 only in the
use of the phrase "shake from dust, *n'r m'pr*"; it is otherwise a call to
Jerusalem to "shake [itself] from the dust" of destruction. Sir 11:12, on
the other hand, refers to Yahweh's salvation of the individual. The lines
from Theognis might seem, in the second place, to contain Ben Sira's
contrast between the one who strives unsuccessfully (v 11) and the
hopeless one to whom God gives success, if one did not quite understand
Theognis's meaning. There one reads, "Sometimes he that striveth to be
of good repute (*ho men eudokimein peirōmenos*) falleth unawares into
ruin great and sore, whereas for the doer of good (*tǭ de kalōs poieunti*)
God maketh good hap in all things, to be his deliverance from folly."
"The contrast lies," however, not between two victims of fate, but
"between the man who does good and the man who tries to seem
good."[44] Theognis, further, clearly makes God's saving action the reward
of goodness, whereas Ben Sira speaks here of God's irrational activity.
Finally, there should be little doubt that Sir 11:12 relies on 1 Sam 2:8
(par. Ps 113:7), "He raises the poor from the dust; he lifts the needy
from the ash heap."

As a parallel to Sir 11:14, "Good and evil, life and death, Poverty and
wealth come from Yahweh," Middendorp gives Theog. 165 (intended is
165–66), "No man living is rich or poor, bad or good, without fortune
(*daimōn*)," and 171 (intended is 171–72), "'Tis certain that without the
Gods man getteth neither good nor ill."[45] The possible influence of
Theognis on Ben Sira would seem more likely here if Middendorp had
not tried to explain the difference between 1 Samuel 2, on the one hand,
and Ben Sira and Theognis, on the other. "For Sir 11:14 one can
certainly think of 1 Samuel 2," he admits, "but there is a small difference: In Hannah's prayer there is the Lord who intrudes into history,
whereas Ben Sira and Theognis think deistically of the cause of the
opposites." Aside, however, from the fact that Ben Sira is certainly not
deistic, the similarity of 11:14 to Hannah's prayer is striking. One may
note especially 1 Sam 2:6–8:

> Yahweh kills and brings to life;
> > he brings down to Sheol and raises up.
> Yahweh makes poor and makes rich;
> > he brings low, he also exalts.
> He raises up the poor from the dust;
> > he lifts the needy from the ash heap.
> . . . .

[43] Ibid., 17.
[44] The comment is that of the editor, Edmonds, in *Elegy and Iambus*, 299 n. 1.
[45] Middendorp, *Stellung*, 17.

> For the pillars of the earth are Yahweh's
> and on them he has set the world.

Where is the *"in die Geschichte eingreifende[r] Herr"* who is to be distinguished from Ben Sira's god in these verses; and why are they any less "deistic" than Ben Sira and Theognis? The *"kleiner Unterschied"* cannot be maintained. Ben Sira's "life and death, poverty and wealth" follow 1 Sam 2:6–7 exactly, and we just saw above that Sir 11:12 relies on 1 Sam 2:8; the connection thus seems certain. Only Ben Sira's "good and evil" are not in 1 Samuel 2, and this could conceivably have been influenced by the "rich or poor, bad or good" of Theog. 165–66; that is to say that I would regard it as possible that Ben Sira, in following and revising the sentiments of 1 Samuel 2, noted that Theog. 165–66 contained a similar and compatible thought and took over "good and evil" from that source. Theognis would hardly be needed for this addition, however, since the universalist author of Isa 45:7 had proclaimed strongly: "I make *peace* and create *iniquity*, I am Yahweh, who do all these things"; and the sentiment may well have become a commonplace of the Jewish proverbial tradition by Ben Sira's time (it is the theme of Job, and Qoheleth's Epicureanism involves a similar view).

Other Greek Authors

If, however, not all the parallels listed by Middendorp between Ben Sira and Theognis are close enough to convince us that borrowing has taken place, still we have seen sufficient convincing parallels to support the conclusion that Ben Sira did, in fact, read and use Theognis in composing his own work. While it would be appropriate to turn now to a discussion of Ben Sira's *manner* of borrowing, of the way in which he made use of Theognis, such a discussion can best be undertaken after we have looked at some of the evidence for Ben Sira's alleged borrowing from other Hellenic authors.

An examination of the parallels listed by Middendorp between Ben Sira and other Hellenic writers does not support the view that Ben Sira read and used any other Hellenic author than Theognis. Middendorp, indeed, makes no such claim, but only that Ben Sira had used a chrestomathy in addition to his use of Theognis.[46] We know that such collections of worthwhile maxims existed in Ben Sira's day;[47] and, if he could use one such collection (Theognis),[48] he could certainly use another. The possibility of such use, however, does not constitute evidence that Ben

[46] Above, p. 29.

[47] Cf. H. J. Rose, *A Handook of Greek Literature from Homer to the Age of Lucian* (New York: Dutton, 1960) 347–50.

[48] Rose, ibid., 347, suggests that Theognis, in the form in which we have the work, is already a collection of maxims.

Sira actually used such a hypothetical work, and an examination of the evidence appears to support the conclusion that he did not.

Middendorp cites only three passages in Ben Sira for which parallels from the *Iliad* are adduced, and only five for which parallels from the *Odyssey* are adduced—already surprising in view of the great esteem in which these works (the "Bible of the Greeks") were held in the Hellenistic age. For the *Iliad* only one parallel is convincing. When Middendorp states flatly that "Sir 14:18 comes from *Il.* 6.148–49,"[49] he is likely correct. In Ben Sira here we have

> As the leaf that groweth on a luxuriant tree,
>> One fadeth, and another sprouteth;
> So (are) the generations of flesh and blood,
>> One dieth, and another flourisheth;[50]

whereas *Il.* 6.146–49 reads,

> As is the generation of leaves, so is that of humanity.
> The wind scatters the leaves on the ground, but the live timber
> burgeons with leaves again in the season of spring returning.
> So one generation of men will grow while another
> dies.[51]

While it might be suggested that any sage anywhere might notice the similarity between dying and new birth in vegetation and dying and new birth among human beings, still the manner of expression and the movement of thought in these two passages is strikingly similar; and one may note further the following verbal connections: Ben Sira's use of *prḥ* corresponds to Homer's use of *telethaō* or *phyō* or both; Ben Sira's use of *'lh* corresponds to Homer's use of *phylla*; Ben Sira's use of *ṣmḥ* corresponds to Homer's use of *phyō*; Ben Sira's use of *dwrwt* corresponds to Homer's use of *geneē*; and Ben Sira's *'ḥd . . . 'ḥd* construction in the last line corresponds to Homer's *men . . . de* construction in the last line, both applied to the "generations." Such similarities could hardly be the result of chance.

The other alleged parallels from the *Iliad*, however, are much less certain. Ben Sira's statement in 4:20–21 about two kinds of shame is not

---

[49] Middendorp, *Stellung*, 19.

[50] *kĕperaḥ 'āleh 'al 'ēṣ ra'ănān   šezzeh nôbēl wĕ'aḥēr ṣômēăḥ.*
ken dôrôt bāśār wādām   'eḥad gôwēă' wĕ'eḥad gômēl.

[51] *hoiē per phyllōn geneē, toiē de kai andrōn.*
phylla ta men t'anemos chamadis cheei, alla de th'hylē
telethoōsa phyei, earos d'epigignetai hōrē:
hōs andrōn geneē hē men phyei, hē d'apolēgei.

Text from *Homeri Ilias* (5th ed.; Leipzig: Teubner, 1888); ET from *The Iliad of Homer* (Phoenix Books; trans. Richmond Lattimore; Chicago and London: Univ. of Chicago Press, 1951).

the same as *Il.* 24.44,[52] since Homer means that being ashamed of an impropriety may lead one to harm oneself in penance, whereas Ben Sira means that improper shame may lead one away from wisdom and righteousness. For Ben Sira to note, further, that wolf and sheep do not normally cohabit (Sir 13:17) is hardly evidence of his use of *Il.* 22.262–66,[53] since, although this might well be a matter of universal observation, he could have learned of the incongruity of such cohabitation from its miraculous reversal in Isa 11:6. Sir 13:17, however, compares wolf and lamb with wicked and righteous, which is not to be found either in *Il.* 22.262–66 or in Isa 11:6; so that the situation here is quite different from that in the case of Sir 14:18 and *Il.* 6.148–49, where the parallelism went quite beyond what might have been universally observed. Here the universally observable phenomenon is the only connection, and the most likely conclusion is that the contrast is independent.

An analysis of the alleged parallels from the *Odyssey* is even less satisfying. As parallel to Sir 11:21cd, "It is easy in Yahweh's sight Suddenly—in a moment—to make a poor man rich," Middendorp cites *Od.* 16.211, where Odysseus observes that "it is a light thing for the gods . . . to glorify any mortal man, or else to degrade him."[54] Middendorp notes especially the coincidence of the word "light" or "easy" (*nkh̠, hrēïdion*), but he also refers again to the prayer of Hannah in 1 Samuel 2, and this is surely the more relevant parallel, for 1 Sam 2:7 refers to rich and poor, whereas the connection with the *Odyssey* is only that of the same general theme and the word "easy." *Od.* 17.217, "like guides what is like itself, just as a god does," indeed expresses the same theme as Sir 13:15: "All flesh loveth its kind, And every man his like,"[55] and the theme does not appear otherwise to be biblical; yet the context is different, since the theme appears as an insult in the *Odyssey* (Odysseus is a beggar and scoundrel by association) but as advice in Ben Sira (the righteous do not associate with the wicked). It would also seem likely that such a theme is universal, and I believe that it would not be incorrect to say that it is at least implied in the frequent admonitions in Proverbs to avoid the company of the wicked and foolish.

As a parallel to Sir 20:22, where Ben Sira again refers to the unfortunate consequences of the wrong kind of shame, Middendorp proposes *Od.* 1.7, "They were destroyed by their own wild recklessness, fools

---

[52] Cf. Middendorp, *Stellung*, 14.

[53] Ibid., 18.

[54] Ibid., 17. Text of *Odyssey* from *Homer's Odyssey* (2 vols.; 2d ed.; Oxford: Clarendon Press, 1886). ET from *The Odyssey of Homer* (trans. Richmond Lattimore; New York, *et al.*: Harper & Row, 1967).

[55] Middendorp, *Stellung*, 18.

(*nēpioi*)",[56] yet even if folly here stood in the same relationship to destruction as does shame in Sir 20:22—which it does not—folly is not shame, and a reliance on the *Odyssey* is most unlikely. The suggestion, further, that Sir 34:9–13, where Ben Sira refers to his travels and their attendant dangers, relies on *Od.* 1.1–10 is far-fetched.[57] For Sir 43:24, "They that go down to the sea tell of its extent," Middendorp refers to Ps 107:23–24, which is surely correct (cf. the further connection with Sir 43:25),[58] but then he adds, "Possibly a reference to Odysseus is intended in addition."[59] How could that be affirmed for such a general statement?

The evidence from the *Iliad* and the *Odyssey*, then, for Ben Sira's alleged use of a chrestomathy other than Theognis is reduced to one quotation, *Il.* 6.146–49. Could one conclude on that basis that Ben Sira used a chrestomathy containing useful sayings from Homer, or even that such a chrestomathy existed? Hardly; the figure of speech comparing human life to leaves on a tree might well have become a common saying by Ben Sira's time, like our earlier misquotations from Shakespeare. The fact that one would be able to find in Homer so many lines that Ben Sira probably would have been able to use casts doubt at this point on the whole theory of his use of such a chrestomathy as that suggested by Middendorp, since, if it existed, it would surely have contained many Homeric sage observations about life, and, if Ben Sira used it, he would almost certainly have used many of those observations.

While it would be a rather thankless endeavor to examine in detail every Hellenic parallel to Ben Sira cited by Middendorp in support of his chrestomathy theory, the alleged parallels with three other authors should be pursued. The author whose works remind Middendorp of one or another line in Ben Sira next most frequently to Theognis is Euripides; yet the nineteen references to Euripides are spread over eleven plays and the *fragmenta incerta*, which inclines me strongly toward the view, especially after our examination of the Homeric evidence, that Ben Sira did not make use of the writings of Euripides in any direct way, either in their original form or in a chrestomathy. A consideration of the first parallel that Middendorp alleges between Euripides and Ben Sira supports the impression. For Sir 3:21–23,

> Seek not (to understand) what is too wonderful for thee,
>   And search not out that which is hid from thee.
> Meditate upon that which *has been permitted thee*,
>   And be not occupied with that which is hid.

---

[56] Ibid., 20.
[57] Ibid., 22.
[58] Cf. the discussion above, pp. 23–24.
[59] Middendorp, *Stellung*, 24.

Have naught to do with[60] that which is beyond thee,
For more hath been shown to thee than thou canst
understand,

Middendorp refers to Ps 131:1,[61] "I do not occupy myself with things too
great and too marvelous for me"; yet he adds that he is also reminded of
Eur. *Bacch.* 390ff. and *Med.* 1225f. There seems, however, no need to
look beyond the Psalm here, although in *Bacch.* 395–99 we do find a
somewhat similar thought: "Knowledge is not wisdom, and considering
immortal things makes a short life. Furthermore, he who pursues
marvelous things may not keep what he has."[62] Ben Sira, of course, does
not include the threat. *Med.* 1225–26 contains merely a jibe at,
apparently, the Sophists (*sophoi dokountes*).[63]

Next to Euripides, the two authors most cited by Middendorp as presenting Hellenic parallels to parts of Ben Sira are Xenophon (thirteen
references to the *Memorabilia*) and Hesiod (eleven references, all save
one to the *Works and Days*), and some attention must now be given to
the alleged parallels between these two authors and Ben Sira. For
Hesiod, the only parallels that will stand up at all under scrutiny are *Op.*
317–19, "An evil shame (*aidōs*) is the needy man's companion, shame
which both greatly harms and prospers men: shame is with poverty
(*anolbiēs*), but confidence (*tharsos*) with wealth (*olbos*),"[64] offered as a
parallel to Sir 4:20–21,

My son, *keep* times *of abundance*, and beware of evil,
And be not ashamed concerning thy soul.
For there is a shame that *is the portion of iniquity*,
And there is a shame (that *is the portion of*) honour and
favour;

and *Op.* 346, "A bad neighbor is as great a plague as a good one is a
great blessing,"[65] offered as a parallel to Sir 6:14b, "He that findeth [a
faithful friend] findeth a treasure." There are problems with both parallels, however. It is questionable at the outset whether any Hellenic reference to *aidōs* is parallel to anything in Ben Sira, since the Hebrew terms
bwš and *bšt* are more nearly what the Greeks meant by *aischynē* and
related words, as is seen in the fact that the LXX usually translates *bšt*
with *aischynē* and never with *aidōs*, and in the further fact that *aidōs*
almost never appears in the LXX at all, even in the originally Greek

---

[60] Literally: "Do not show disobedience regarding . . ."
[61] Middendorp, *Stellung*, 13.
[62] Text in *The Bacchae of Euripides* (Cambridge: Univ. Press, 1900); my translation.
[63] Text in *Euripides, Medea* (Oxford: Univ. Press, 1969).
[64] Middendorp, *Stellung*, 14; cited is only line 317. Text and ET of Hesiod from *Hesiod,
the Homeric Hymns, and Homerica* (LCL; Cambridge, Mass.: Harvard Univ. Press, 1967).
[65] Middendorp, *Stellung*, 15.

works. *Aidōs* thus represents a concept that is un-Hebraic. In any case, Hesiod means to say that shame has both advantages and disadvantages, whereas confidence is more reliable; this is not Ben Sira's meaning.[66] While there is some similarity, finally, between Ben Sira's friend as "treasure (*hwn*)" and Hesiod's friend as "blessing (*oneiar*)," it must be borne in mind that we are in the midst of a section of Ben Sira in which he has relied heavily on Theognis, and that Sir 6:14–15 bears a striking similarity to Theog. 77.[67]

Other alleged parallels in Hesiod for Ben Sira do not ring true. Sir 11:18–19, where Ben Sira points out that death separates one from one's riches, is hardly the same as *Op.* 320–25, where Hesiod refers to the destruction of those who seize wealth "violently and perforce."[68] Ben Sira expresses here his recurring theme that all the gains and possessions of life must be left behind at death (only one's good name remaining), whereas Hesiod refers to hybris and nemesis. Regarding Sir 27:27, "He that doeth evil things, they shall roll upon him," to take a final alleged parallel from Hesiod, Middendorp observes, "Thus Hesiod expresses himself, *Op.* 265f.,"[69] where one may read, "He does mischief to himself who does mischief to another, and evil planned harms the plotter most." Ben Sira here, however, without a doubt relies on Prov 26:27, "He who digs a pit will fall into it, and a stone will come back upon him who starts it rolling." He has reworked the stone saying in v 25 and has quoted the stich about the pit in v 26. Verse 27 is merely an expansion of the theme, whereby Ben Sira probably plays on the stone image of the second stich of Prov 26:27.[70]

The case for meaningful parallels can be made rather better with regard to Xenophon's *Memorabilia*. Regarding Sir 1:25, Middendorp notes that "the expression 'treasures of wisdom' also occurs in Xenophon *Mem.* 4.2.9."[71] That is correct.[72] Also, for the phrase "in word and in deed" in Sir 3:8, he cites several places in the *Memorabilia*, noting that such a distinction is not consonant with the Old Testament *dbr*.[73] In *Mem.* 2.3.8 Chaerecrates says to Socrates that he knows how "to speak well to one who speaks well and to do good to one who does good

---

[66] The contrast between shame and confidence is to be found elsewhere in Greek literature; cf. Plato, *Laws* 647A–649C.

[67] Cf. above, p. 31.

[68] Middendorp, *Stellung*, 17.

[69] Ibid., 21.

[70] Segal, *Spr Bn Syr'*, apparently so takes it and gives for Sir 27:27a *'ôśeh ra' 'ēlāyw yāśûb*; cf. Prov 26:27b, *gōlēl 'eben 'ēlāyw tāśûb*. Cf. further above, p. 4–5, and n. 6.

[71] Middendorp, *Stellung*, 13.

[72] Text and ET of the *Memorabilia* from Xenophon, *Memorabilia and Oeconomicus* (LCL; New York: G. P. Putnam's Sons, 1923).

[73] Middendorp, *Stellung*, 13.

(*epistamenos ge kai eu legein ton eu legonta kai eu poiein ton eu poiounta*)";[74] and in 2.3.15 he notes that it is normal "that the senior . . . should always act and speak first (*hēgeisthai . . . kai ergou kai logou*)." In 2.3.17 we again have the phrase "words and actions (*kai logos kai ergon*)"; and we have *logos* and *ergon* in similar constructions in 2.10.6 and 3.11.10. Thus there is good evidence for Xenophon's use of such phraseology as probably representative of at least one style of Greek speech. Whether there is anything *inherently* un-Hebraic in the phrase would be another question, although Ben Sira's use of it (the Hebrew is *bm'mr wbm'śh*) may represent a neologism in Hebrew. Professor Gordis has pointed out to me that God is called *'wmr w'wśh* in "the old prayer of the Jewish Morning service *barukh še 'amar*."[75]

For Sir 3:21–23 Middendorp gives as parallels not only Ps 131:1 and Eur. *Med.* 1225–26,[76] but also *Mem.* 1.1.11–12. While the Socratic ideal here described does coincide with Ben Sira's advice to "seek not (to understand) what is too wonderful for thee," one has to recall, nevertheless, that the advice is also biblical, and that it is extremely difficult to argue for Hellenic influence in such a case.

Again in Ben Sira's section on friendship in chap. 6, Middendorp finds *Mem.* 2.6.1 relevant for Sir 6:7, "If thou *acquirest* a friend *acquire him by testing.*"[77] While Ben Sira has relied, as we saw, on Theognis in this section, a convincing parallel from Theognis for this testing of the friend could not be offered; but Xenophon does, indeed, present similarities, since he refers to "testing the qualities that make a man's friendship worth winning (*dokimazein philous hopoious axion ktasthai*)." Thus we have not only testing of a friend but precisely the testing of a new friend.

It is perhaps possible that Sir 7:14, "*Do not give counsel* in the assembly of *princes*," has been prompted by Xenophon's story about Socrates' counsel to Glaucon, who, "though he was less than twenty years old," kept speaking in the Assembly (*Mem.* 3.6.1);[78] but Ben Sira's advice seems to have a more oriental setting (stay away from rulers, cf. Prov 25:6), whereas Glaucon exhibited the folly of rash youth, which is not Ben Sira's theme here. If a connection is to be made, further, between the self-praise of Wisdom in Ben Sira 24 and the speeches of Dame Vice and Dame Virtue to Heracles in *Mem.* 2.1.21–34,[79] then one can only note that the same connection can be made with Proverbs 8–9, so that any reliance on Xenophon here would be impossible to

---

[74] My translation.
[75] In correspondence.
[76] Above, p. 41–42.
[77] Middendorp, *Stellung*, 14.
[78] Ibid., 15–16.
[79] Ibid., 20–21.

demonstrate.[80] The other alleged parallels from Xenophon are even less apt than those discussed here, and we may conveniently pass over them.

Has Ben Sira relied on the *Memorabilia*, or on lines from it quoted in a chrestomathy? I would be inclined to say that he has not. We have only two phrases ("treasures of Wisdom" and "word and deed") and one line (the testing of a new friend) which can be cited as meaningful parallels, all of which can readily be explained on the assumption that such phraseology had simply passed into the mainstream of Hellenistic speech by Ben Sira's day—if, indeed, Xenophon does not in these cases merely repeat what was already common parlance.

Beyond the writers here discussed, Middendorp refers, for parallels to Ben Sira, to seven lines or passages from Sophocles and five from Aristophanes, and to between one and four passages from each of about two dozen other Greek authors; and these other alleged parallels have about the same degree of correspondence to Ben Sira, upon examination, as those that have been discussed here. One may therefore conclude that Ben Sira may well have relied to some degree on Theognis, but that he did not consciously rely on any other Greek author, whose works he might have known either in their original form or contained in a chrestomathy like that of Theognis. This does not mean that we do not see other evidences of the influence of Hellenic literature in Ben Sira. The Homeric simile of the leaves and human life and the phrases from Xenophon are evidence of such influence; but here we must speak of Ben Sira's unconscious use of Hellenic material, of material that has entered into the mainstream of Hellenistic thinking and speech, that is part of the "Hellenistic diffusion," to return to Hadas's phrase. When we come to discuss the *way* in which Ben Sira has taken over Hellenic material, these two different types of "reliance" will have to remain clearly distinguished. Before that issue can be considered, however, two final complexes of "parallel" material need to be examined.

Hellenistic Veneration of Isis

Middendorp cites with approval Hans Conzelmann's attempt to show a relation between the self praise of Wisdom in Ben Sira 24 and the genre of the Isis hymn.[81] In his article on the subject, Conzelmann states flatly that Sir 24:"3–6(7) are nothing but a hymn to Isis, taken up

---

[80] On Ben Sira 24, cf. further below, pp. 45–50.

[81] Middendorp, *Stellung*, 20; H. Conzelmann, "The Mother of Wisdom," *The Future of Our Religious Past* (ed. James M. Robinson; New York, *et al.*: Harper & Row, 1971) 230–43. Conzelmann was not the first to suggest that Sir 24:3–6 relied on Isis aretalogies. Cf., e.g., H. Ringgren, *Word and Wisdom* (Lund: Håkan Ohlssons Boktryckeri, 1947) 146. A view nearer that argued here was maintained by U. Wilckens, "sophia, ktl.," *TDNT* 7. 509.

almost literally and retouched lightly at only one or two points," and, in order to substantiate this claim, he first seeks to show that there is "nothing specifically Jewish" in Sir 24:3–6.[82] His first point is that "the first person is characteristic of the Wisdom-songs" (I believe that he means, e.g., Proverbs 8–9) "just as it is of the Isis-aretalogies."[83] If a trait is in Proverbs, however, how can one call it not "specifically Jewish" as far as Ben Sira is concerned? Next Conzelmann mentions that *homichlē* ("mist," v 3) might remind one of Gen 1:2 but that the word is not there; yet surely the mere absence of a word is not firm evidence if similar ideas are present, which they are. Then Conzelmann advances the notion that "*abyssos* occurs in Gen. 1, but embedded in a different (and moreover quite non-Jewish) worldview." Here he appears to want to taint the evidence; in other words, if a term or concept appears in Sir 24:3–6 which Conzelmann can find in the Isis aretalogies but which also occurs in the Bible, he wants to undercut the Jewishness of the occurrence in the Bible by arguing that it is not Jewish there. That the creation story of Genesis 1 bears remarkably Babylonian traits, however, is no argument that it was not Jewish in Ben Sira's day! The Torah was, in the Hellenistic period, quintessentially Jewish; but Conzelmann seems to overlook that fact. How the world view differs, in any case, escapes me, since both in Gen 1:2 and in Sir 24:5 we have to do with the primordial abyss that existed before the differentiation of creation. Perhaps Conzelmann means that the Wisdom of God does not appear in Genesis 1, but the Spirit of God does, and the two were probably widely identified in Ben Sira's day, as Box and Oesterley already noted,[84] and as Georg Ziener has shown in detail.[85]

Conzelmann continues by noting that, although Ben Sira uses the term "most high (*hypsistos*)" in 24:2, 23, the term is also "a typical expression of the syncretistic situation, and in any case the work is a catchword of the [Isis] aretalogies." I simply do not know what to make of this point. The word *'lywn*, which is surely the original here (Segal writes it for vv 3, 23 but prefers *'lwhym*, for v 2), is used alone in the extant Hebrew portions of Ben Sira twenty times, and nineteen of these occurrences are in chaps. 30–50, which are the most specifically Jewish part of the book! To these one will have to add the likely uses of *'lywn* in all those other places, such as chap. 24, for which the Hebrew has not survived but where the Greek writes *hypsistos*. Had Conzelmann, furthermore, consulted a concordance to the LXX, he might have noted the

[82] Conzelmann, "Mother," 235.

[83] This and the following "proofs" of the non-Judaic character of Sir 24:3–6 (7) are given ibid., n. 27.

[84] ad Sir 24:3.

[85] G. Ziener, *Die theologische Begriffssprache im Buche der Weisheit* (BBB 11; Bonn: Peter Hanstein, 1956).

great frequency of the term *hypsistos* and might thus never have tried to imply that there was anything un-Judaic in the use of the term. That *hypsistos* appears in two of the Isis aretalogies is, then, insignificant in the light of the Judaic evidence.

The last "non-Jewish" trait indicated by Conzelmann is the phrase, "pillar of cloud," v 4, which he describes as possibly "a retouching occasioned by Exodus. But not a word of the text recalls the history of Israel. Furthermore, the pillar here is cosmic. So the motif is not of biblical origin." Yet if one were to put into juxtaposition the statements of Prov 8:27a and 28a, which refer to Wisdom's presence or participation in the creation of the heavens, and Prov 9:1, where Wisdom's seven pillars are set up—and Ben Sira very well might, of course, have juxtaposed these verses because of their proximity in the Bible—one might produce such a statement as that of Sir 24:4. Be that as it may, however, the lines which secure the Jewishness of the verse are Job 26:10–11: "He has described a circle upon the face of the waters [cf. Prov 8:27: "I was there, when he drew a circle on the face of the deep"]. . . . The pillars of heaven tremble." Conzelmann, then, has not produced a single non-Judaic term or concept in the alleged "lightly retouched" Isis hymn of Ben Sira 24.[86]

Conzelmann next moves to an attempt to show that most of the elements of Sir 24:3–6(7) have parallels *either* in one or more of the Isis aretalogies *or* elsewhere in Egyptian literature, even of a much more ancient period. These may be discussed briefly, but we should pause here to note what Conzelmann finally admits, namely that there is no Isis hymn known to him which Ben Sira has quoted "almost literally and retouched lightly"; rather, he is dealing with a reconstructed hymn,[87] reconstructed, in fact, on the basis of Sir 24:3–6(7), parallels for various aspects of which he finds in Egyptian literature, especially in the collection of Isis aretalogies. His argument is thus half tautological, the other half resting on the argument that these verses in Ben Sira are *not* Jewish but *are* similar to Isis/Egyptian religious statements. We have already seen that Conzelmann's evidence for the non-Judaic character of the passage is invalid; it thus remains to examine whether his Egyptian parallels are necessary in the light of the Judaic tradition about the Wisdom of God.

Conzelmann is right in observing that the statement that Wisdom "came forth from the mouth" of God is an Egyptian trait.[88] But "the

---

[86] Crenshaw, *Wisdom*, 155, lists "creation by the divine word; the creative mist . . . ; the pillar of cloud . . . ; the sacred tent . . . ; [and] Israel as God's special possession" as elements of "traditional matter" in Ben Sira 24.

[87] Conzelmann, "Mother," 239.

[88] Ibid., 235.

antithesis between 'above' and 'below'" is the same in Prov 8:26-27 as in
Sir 24:5;[89] and Sir 24:4-6 does not present the contrast that Conzelmann
finds in Egyptian literature between the "abiding" nature of a "primal
God" and the "movement" of Isis,[90] since what Ben Sira expresses here is
that Wisdom was actively present everywhere, just as in Prov 8:24-31.
Conzelmann, however, takes Wisdom's "walking the circuit of the
world" (v 5, "I encompassed the circuit of heaven") to mean that she
created and rules the cosmos,[91] and he briskly brushes aside the parallel
in Proverbs to these verses in Ben Sira by stating that "we may ignore
here the question of whether or not in Prov 8:22ff. Wisdom is
Creator."[92] But the situation is virtually the same in Sir 24:3-6 as in Prov
8:22-29, in both of which Wisdom's role as creatrix is a teasing possibility but is not explicitly stated. This point has been made especially well
by Maurice Gilbert,[93] to whose study of the subject I want to return
below. Wisdom does become ruler of the cosmos in Sir 24:6; and Conzelmann may have a possible connection with Isis theology here. Ben Sira
seems consciously to revise Prov 8:31, which has Wisdom "rejoicing in
his *created* world and delighting in the sons of men," since Ben Sira has
Wisdom say, "*in* the waves of the sea, and *in* all the earth, And *among*
every people and nation I held sway." If there is an Egyptian connection
here, however, it seems to be more linguistic than conceptual, since Ben
Sira specifically removes the ambiguity of Proverbs 8 by having Wisdom
refer, in 24:8, to God as "the Creator of all things."

   It is not clear what Conzelmann intends to show by referring to the
Egyptian "circuit" that is "traversed," which "includes both the upper
and the lower world," in other words the "unity in tension."[94] The circle
in Prov 8:27 is "on the face of the deep" and in Job 26:10 "of the
waters"; whereas in Sir 24:5 the circle is astronomical, and Wisdom
walks "in the depth of the abyss." We therefore have something of a
reversal of imagery in Ben Sira from that of Job and Proverbs, where the
circle of the deep is put over against the "pillars of heaven" (Job 26:11)
or Yahweh's making "firm the skies above" (Prov 8:28). I take the difference in expression to be due to the widespread interest in astrology in
Ben Sira's day, which has provided the concept of the circle of the heavens; but there is no essential difference between Ben Sira and Proverbs at
this point. Both affirm that the Wisdom of God was created first and that
she dwelt both above and below.

[89] Conzelmann, ibid., 236, offers Egyptian parallels.
[90] Ibid. I think that the contrast, in any case, is more Hellenic than Egyptian; Conzelmann's source at this point is Plutarch.
[91] Conzelmann, "Mother," 229.
[92] Ibid., n. 31.
[93] M. Gilbert, "L'éloge de la Sagesse (*Siracide* 24)," *RTL* 5 (1974) 344-45.
[94] Conzelmann, "Mother," 237.

It is not necessary to refer, as Conzelmann does, to the Isis aretalogies or to Egyptian literature for the statement in Ben Sira that
Wisdom is "alone" (v 5), or for the implication that "she *knows* all and
can provide instruction about it" (he draws the implication from v 5), or
for her association with the sea.[95] Only the word "alone" is missing from
Wisdom's solitude in Prov 8:22–26; Wisdom's teaching is quite explicit
in Prov 8:32–36; and the association of Wisdom with the sea is exactly
the same in Ben Sira 24 as in Proverbs 8. On the basis of the above
observations, however, Conzelmann then suggests that initiation into a
mystery is implied in our text, since the Isis/Wisdom who alone knows
all things can impart this knowledge to initiates.[96] Against such a
suggestion one can only observe that there is no hint of a mystery in Ben
Sira 24, and that Wisdom is immediately (v 23, but already by implication in v 8) identified with Torah.[97] The place of this identification in
Ben Sira's system has already been discussed above, but one may note
here further that Prov 8:32–36, on which Ben Sira directly relies at this
point, refers to an open and not to a guarded teaching.

When Conzelmann finds the theme that Wisdom displays her power
both in the cosmos and in the human sphere also in the Isis aretalogies,[98]
he has of course ignored the presence of just this theme in Proverbs 8.
Finally, Conzelmann wants to find influence from the Isis literature in
the following section of Ben Sira, Sir 24:8–34, in which Wisdom is identified with Torah. He refers to the theme of Isis as law giver and
observes that "the uniform viewpoint is Right, Truth, Order, i.e.,
Maat."[99] Yet in Ben Sira 24 Wisdom is not a law giver, but rather *is* the
law; and other aspects of Ma'at—truth and order—are precisely missing
from Ben Sira 24.[100]

While Conzelmann's hypothesis of an Isis hymn in Sir 24:3–6, therefore, has almost no verifiable evidence at all to support it, his last
suggested parallel has touched upon the issue that allows us to say what
is actually going on in Sir 24:3–6—that is, that Wisdom is being
identified with Torah. If we bear in mind that one of Ben Sira's main
theological emphases was this identification of *traditional* wisdom with
traditional Torah, we should not be surprised that he also, in chap. 24,

---

[95] Ibid., 238.

[96] Ibid.

[97] I cannot agree with Crenshaw, *Wisdom*, 169, that Ben Sira has, by this identification,
"squelched" the mythical side of Wisdom. He has rather elevated the Torah to primordial
status; cf. further immediately below.

[98] Conzelmann, "Mother," 239.

[99] Ibid., 241.

[100] P. W. Skehan, "Structures in Poems on Wisdom: Proverbs 8 and Sirach 24," *CBQ* 41
(1979) 366, states flatly that Ben Sira 24 "is patterned on [Proverbs 8], in its theme, in its
length, and with echoes in its language." A detailed comparison appears on p. 377.

identified a peculiar aspect of that traditional wisdom—namely the hypostatized Wisdom of Prov 8:22–31—with Torah as well. This relationship between Sir 24:3–6 and Prov 8:22–31 has also been emphasized by Gilbert in the aforementioned study, who goes so far as to assert that the earlier verses in Ben Sira 24, while being "inspired" by Proverbs 8,[101] at the same time recall the Torah *in its order*. Thus not only does there exist a connection between Sir 24:3, at the beginning of the eulogy, and the first verses of Genesis (denied by Conzelmann but true nevertheless), but also Sir 24:23, where Wisdom is explicitly identified with Torah, quotes the end of the Torah, Deut 33:4 ("the Law which Moses commanded *us* (as) an heritage for the assemblies of Jacob").[102] When Gilbert goes further to find the chronological order from the Torah— "universal origins," "the election of Israel," and "the centralization of the cult"—also in Ben Sira's order in Sir 24:3–6, 7–8, and 10–12 respectively, he has perhaps overstated his case; nevertheless, Gilbert has helped us to understand that there is no direct connection between Ben Sira 24 and any Isis aretalogy, but rather that Ben Sira is here quite systematicallly proceeding in his intention to bring every aspect of traditional Judaic wisdom into harmony with the Torah. It is as he said in 1:26–27: "If thou desire Wisdom, keep the commandments, And the Lord will give her freely unto thee. For the fear of the Lord is wisdom and *training*."[103]

Stoicism

We turn now to the question of Stoic influence on Ben Sira, a question that is extremely difficult for two reasons. In the first place, no Stoic texts survive from the third century, the early period of the school, so that one cannot discuss the possibility of literary relationships, as we have done down to this point. Furthermore, as every student of Stoicism since Max Pohlenz, at least, should have realized, "the Stoa had grown up on Semitic ground, and had a great deal in common with the thought-world of the Old Testament."[104] As Pohlenz put it, "It is certainly not too bold to conclude that the conception of God to be found in Zeno and Chrysippus displays features which have been taken

---

[101] Gilbert, "L'éloge de la Sagesse," 346.
[102] Ibid., 345. Cf. also the brief discussion in R. Gordis, *The Book of God and Man. A Study of Job* (Chicago and London: Univ. of Chicago Press, 1965) 36–37.
[103] Duesberg et Auvray, *Ecclésiastique*, 13–14, also emphasize the identification of Wisdom and Torah in chap. 24. Cf. also Smend, *Weisheit*, XXIII. Cf. also now B. Vawter, "Prov 22: Wisdom and Creation," *JBL* 99 (1980) 206; Vawter is also generally sceptical of the view that Ma'at lies behind the Judaic hypostatized Wisdom. On this point cf. further W. McKane, *Proverbs. A New Approach* (Old Testament Library; Philadelphia: Westminster, 1970) 269–70, 344.
[104] M. Hengel, *Judaism and Hellenism* (Philadelphia: Fortress, 1974) 1. 149.

over from the Orient."[105] In addition to these problems, it must also be borne in mind that formal Stoicism was relatively new in Ben Sira's day, having been founded in Athens by Zeno in about 300, and still, during what must have been Ben Sira's formative years, under its third "head" (prostatēs), Chrysippus (232–207).[106] To what degree will formal and specific teachings of the school have spread to a backwater of the Ptolemaic empire (Jerusalem) by this time? While that question cannot be answered in any definitive way, it must be raised as a reminder that the issue of Stoic influence on Ben Sira must be handled with extreme caution.

Raymond Pautrel, who is aware of at least the first of the problems just defined,[107] has attempted to bring clarity to the issue.[108] After finding that Sir 40:28, "My son, live not a beggar's life; Better is one dead than importunate," repeats the Stoic polemic against Cynicism,[109] Pautrel tries to show that three of the major philosophical and theological positions of the early Stoa are to be found in Ben Sira: human dignity, the unity of the world, and the unity of humanity.[110] As examples of Ben Sira's interest in human dignity, Pautrel cites especially those texts that most commentators label eudaemonistic, e.g., 15:6, "Joy and gladness shall he [who fears Yahweh] find, And [Wisdom] will make him inherit an everlasting name," and also Ben Sira's paramount interest in shame.[111] For the unity of the cosmos, he of course cites Sir 43:27, "The conclusion of the matter is: He is all," as well as what he calls an "optimism of reason" in 39:16–35:[112] "The works of God are all good, and he supplies every need in its season" (vv 16, 33), etc. Finally, for the unity of humanity, Pautrel points to Ben Sira's hope for the conversion of the Gentiles in 36:5: "That they may know, as we also know, That there is none other God but Thee."[113] There is something less than convincing about these three connections, however, and Pautrel admits that certitude is impossible.[114]

Most students of Ben Sira would hardly conclude that his eudaemonism and his interest in shame proceded from a Stoic-like concept of

---

[105] M. Pohlenz, Die Stoa (3d ed.; Göttingen: Vandenhoeck & Ruprecht, 1964) 1. 108. ET in Hengel, Judaism and Hellenism, 1.149.

[106] Oxford Classical Dictionary (2d ed.; 1970) 1015.

[107] Page 540 of the article cited in the following note.

[108] R. Pautrel, "Ben Sira et le stoïcisme," RSR 51 (1963) 535–49.

[109] Ibid., 539.

[110] Ibid., 541. Middendorp, Stellung, 28–29, "underscores" this position. Cf. also J. Marböck, Weisheit im Wandel. Untersuchungen zur Weisheitstheologie bei Ben Sira (BBB 37; Bonn: Peter Hanstein, 1971) 170–71, who agrees generally with Pautrel.

[111] Pautrel, "Stoïcisme," 541.

[112] Ibid., 543.

[113] Ibid., 546.

[114] Ibid., 547.

human dignity. Self-interest lies at the core of the proverbial wisdom tradition, as the repeated admonition of Prov 4:4 and 7:2, "Keep my commandments, and live," makes clear; the good life is indeed the goal of the sage. Ben Sira's pronounced interest in shame and one's good name have been discussed above, but we need to remind ourselves here that Ben Sira's goal of the preservation of one's good name is his way of going beyond his tradition to something that he considered more profound than the mere interest in life, to something, indeed, that approaches immortality. It is as he says in 41:13, "*The value of a* life lasts for *a number of* days, But the *value* of a name for days without number." In any case, human dignity is firmly fixed in the Bible, cf. Psalm 8.

There is no doubt that Sir 43:27 is, taken alone, a pantheistic statement, and that it is reminiscent of the Stoic *Allmachtsformeln* analyzed by Eduard Norden. No one, of course, thinks that Ben Sira endorses pantheism, if for no other reason than that he states in v 28, "Greater is He than all His works"; and Ben Sira's statement in v 27 is not in the traditional form of an *Allmachtsformel*, which usually takes a form something like that given by Seneca, who quotes Plato to the effect that the causes are *id ex quo, id a quo, id in quo, id ad quod, id propter quod, novissime id quod ex his est*.[115] (Other versions of the formula are related, by Stoic writers, to the world and the creator.) Does the statement, "He is all," reveal Stoic influence? It is possible, but it is equally possible that such statements may simply have been current and widespread in Ben Sira's day, the result of growing philosophical monotheism.[116]

Also, for the view of Sir 39:16–35 that all of God's creation is good and purposeful and that nothing has been created without purpose, one need hardly go beyond the Bible and the wisdom tradition. Gen 1:1–2:4a reiterates the goodness of creation and clearly implies both God's provision for his creatures and the purposefulness of every created thing, although the last is not explicitly stated. One might even say that such an implication is so strong in Genesis 1 that Sir 39:34, "None may say: This is *evil; what is it?* For everything *displayeth strength* in its season," accurately expresses a part of the theology upon which Genesis 1 rests! One may cite further, however, Ps 33:6, 9:

> By the word of Yahweh the heavens were made,
>   and all their host by the breath of his mouth.

---

[115] Sen. *Ep.* 65.8; cited in M. Dibelius, *An die Kolosser Epheser an Philemon* (HNT; 3d ed.; ed. Heinrich Greeven; Tübingen: Mohr [Siebeck], 1953) 13.

[116] There may well also be some kind of connection between Sir 43:27 and Qoh 12:13. Cf. on this possibility Middendorp, *Stellung*, 89.

> For he spoke, and it came to be;
>   he commanded, and it stood forth,

or Ps 147:8–9:

> He covers the heavens with clouds,
>   he prepares rain for the earth,
>   he makes grass grow upon the hills.
> He gives to the beasts their food,
>   and to the young ravens which cry.

If Pautrel argues that the central issue here for Ben Sira and for the early Stoics was the "unity and the intelligibility of the world," i.e., the world's susceptibility to being understood rationally,[117] then one will have to reply that such was always the presupposition of the Jewish sages; especially Prov 24:3, from the oldest layer of the Book of Proverbs, may be cited as exhibiting this confidence in reason: "By wisdom a house is built, and by understanding it is established."

For the unity of all humanity under one god one may refer again to Psalm 8 and also, especially in this case, to Deutero-Isaiah. That there was only one god, that all human beings were his proper subjects, and that he had created all, both good and evil, were cardinal points in the theology of the Second Isaiah. So frequently do these points occur in Deutero-Isaiah that it is almost gratuitous to cite any one passage, but perhaps the moving address to Cyrus, 45:5–7, may be quoted here as a reminder that universalistic monotheism was not new with the Stoics:

> I am Yahweh, and there is no other,
>   besides me there is no God;
>   I gird you, though you do not know me,
> that men may know, from the rising of the sun
>   and from the west, that there is none besides me;
>   I am Yahweh, and there is no other.
> I form light and create darkness,
>   I make *peace* and create *evil*,
>   I am Yahweh, who do all these things.

Pautrel recognizes the universalistic tendency in the prophets but asks why Ben Sira chooses, as he puts it, the Nineveh of Jonah over the Nineveh of Tobit if it is not because of the universalistic emphasis provided to the age by the early Stoa. The question would be impossible to answer in that form, but one must underscore that Ben Sira's universalism is inherently Judaic. He identifies Wisdom and Torah and states that Wisdom/Torah was offered to the world but was accepted only in Israel (24:7–8), and his hope for the Gentiles is that they will be converted

---

117 Pautrel, "Stoïcisme," 543.

(36:1–5, a passage which Pautrel cites as evidence of Ben Sira's Stoic-like universalism).[118]

It thus appears that only in the case of the statement, "He is all," can a reliance on Stoicism be plausibly suggested; and even here Ben Sira does not use the statement in a Stoic way.[119]

Greek Themes and Terms

Middendorp also listed other Hellenistic themes and vocabulary which he thought could be found in Ben Sira, without reference to particular Hellenic authors.[120] Here, however, the discussion either is too general to be of any help or is simply mistaken. He thinks, for example, that the Hellenic concept of *syneidēsis*, conscience, appears in Sir 13:25–26 in the term *lb*, heart.[121] But Ben Sira writes here,

> The heart of a man changeth his countenance,
> 　　Whether for good or for evil.
> The outcome of a happy heart is a cheerful countenance,

almost certainly drawn from Prov 15:13: "A glad heart makes a *happy* countenance." Again, Middendorp suggests that Ben Sira's term *mwsr* reflects the conceptuality of the Hellenic *paideia*,[122] a notion which could be suggested only by someone who has not consulted a Hebrew concordance on the word *mwsr* for the Book of Proverbs; and he finds *aretē* behind the phrase *ṭwbt šm*,[123] which is extremely unlikely in view of Ben Sira's characteristic views with regard to the importance of the name.[124]

Middendorp also thinks that Ben Sira's organization of proverbs around themes, in something like chapters, as well as his giving his name as that of the author are Hellenic themes.[125] While such connections may appear plausible, these traits are actually drawn from Egyptian wisdom literature, as will become amply clear below in chap. 3.

The foregoing analysis has shown that the only Hellenic writer used directly and consciously by Ben Sira was Theognis, but that he has also occasionally employed an image or saying which probably originated

---

[118] Ibid., 546.

[119] R. E. Murphy, "Hebrew Wisdom," *JAOS* 101 (1981) 24, sees the influence on Ben Sira of "biblical tradition"; but he also takes over too easily, in reliance on Pautrel and Middendorp, the conclusion of "the influence of Hellenism."

[120] Middendorp, *Stellung*, 26–28.

[121] Ibid., 27.

[122] Ibid., 28.

[123] Ibid.

[124] Cf. above, pp. 17–18.

[125] Middendorp, *Stellung*, 26–27. That the use of titles was taken over from Greek usage had earlier been suggested by Lévi, *Ecclésiastique* 1 (1898) XXV.

with one or another Hellenic writer. It is now appropriate to give attention to the manner in which Ben Sira has taken over this material. What was his intent in borrowing from a Hellenic writer, and how has Hellenic material affected his Jewish perspective?

Ben Sira's Manner of Borrowing

We see, in fact, that our sage has used his Hellenic material in several different ways. I should like right away to dismiss the unconscious use of Hellenic sayings and idioms, such as the saying about human life being like that of leaves, which derives from the *Iliad*, or the "word and deed" sayings which one finds expressed in Xenophon. Even though such sayings and expressions represent Hellenistic modification of traditional Judaic conceptuality in the direction of Hellenic thought modes, they play a very minor role in Ben Sira's work and, indeed, in his thought. They represent what Martin Hengel calls "echoes" of Hellenic thought (and not "parallels"), of which he says that "we can hardly talk here of a real 'influence'"; rather, one should assume "the transmigration of sayings from gnomic Greek thought . . . by word of mouth."[126] Hengel here refers to *all* the Hellenic parallels; and in this, of course, as we have seen, he is mistaken (I believe that he did not look at the Theognis parallels individually himself). Regarding Ben Sira's unconscious use of Hellenic material, however, we must concur with Hengel's judgment; Ben Sira's work would not be appreciably altered if it were not there.[127]

The matter is different regarding Theognis, whom Ben Sira uses in four distinct ways. In the first instance, he uses Theognis material to expand themes which he inherits from the Judaic proverbial tradition; this is true especially of his use of Theognis's observations about friendship (above pp. 30–31). He will also make use of a Hellenic statement if he thinks that it offers practical advice that carries out the implications of what we usually call the ethical Torah—as opposed to the ritual

---

[126] Hengel, *Judaism and Hellenism*, 1. 149–50.

[127] Ben Sira's free will statements in 15:11–20, which may be contrasted to his deterministic statements in, e.g., 16:26–28, would belong here if D. Winston, "Freedom and Determinism in Greek Philosophy and Jewish Hellenistic Wisdom," *Studia Philonica* 2 (1973) 40–50, were correct in his argument that it is only against the background of the Hellenistic discussion of this problem that the contrast in Ben Sira is to be understood, since the earlier wisdom tradition had been uniformly deterministic. Unfortunately, however, the collection in Proverbs 10–22 already contains just this contrast. Whereas Prov 22:2 expresses the deterministic view: "The rich and the poor meet together; Yahweh is the maker of them all," Prov 11:5 poses the opposite viewpoint: "The righteousness of the blameless keeps his way straight, but the wicked falls by his own wickedness (*běrišʿatô yippōl*)." The presence of such opposite expressions in a wisdom book is rather to be understood on the principle of the observation of opposite circumstances, as von Rad, *Wisdom in Israel*, 247–51, has explained.

aspect of the Torah. Here we may include his use of Theognis's saying on non-retaliation against a neighbor (above, p. 32), which appears to pick up the theme of Lev 19:17–18 ("neighbor").

More in preponderance, however, is Ben Sira's use of Hellenic material that gives practical advice adding detail to his ethics of caution, and also his use of Hellenic material that simply offers sage observations with which Ben Sira agrees. In this last category, we see the sage operating at the most primitive or elemental level of his profession.[128] When we thus see him taking from Theognis, for example, the observation that there is nothing to be gained from acts of beneficence toward the wicked (above, p. 32), we simply see Ben Sira's observations about life which he has happened to find written down somewhere (in Theognis). He is thus carrying out the function of the sage that he described so well in 39:1cd–2a as that of one "who searcheth out the wisdom of all the ancients, And is occupied with the prophets; Who heedeth the discourses of men of renown." (The allusion to the *Iliad's* human generations like leaves of a tree, by the way, might also be listed here, however unconsciously Ben Sira borrows from that work.)

Finally, then, we have those Hellenic sayings which seem to Ben Sira to support his ethics of caution.[129] Here one may cite the saying about caution in speech in 9:18 (above, p. 31)—a theme which, to be sure, also appears strongly in the Book of Proverbs—and especially 31:25–31, the section in which he advises caution and, indeed, moderation in drinking (above, pp. 34–35). Thus has Ben Sira utilized his Hellenic source.

Middendorp tried to show that Ben Sira deliberately chose Hellenic sayings that would be known to his readers and that were identical with—or could be identified with—the Judaic concepts he was expressing. In this way, Ben Sira is supposed to have sought to promote a certain fusion between Judaic and "Hellenistic" thought.[130] Pautrel is also inclined toward the same explanation of Ben Sira's alleged use of Stoic material.[131] Were it Ben Sira's intention, however, to promote a fusion of Judaic and Hellenic thinking, one might expect that he would have been more straightforward about his intention instead of being so subtle and perhaps even devious. Furthermore, this explanation of Ben Sira's intention is very difficult to maintain in view of his pronounced

---

[128] This is the level which von Rad has called "wisdom deriving from experience" ("*Erfahrungsweisheit*") or "empirical and gnomic wisdom" ("*empirisch-gnomische Weisheit*"); cf. his *Old Testament Theology* (New York and Evanston: Harper & Row, 1962), 1. 418–41, esp. p. 421.

[129] Cf. again above, p. 17.

[130] Cf. above, p. 29.

[131] Pautrel, "Stoïcisme," 545–46, notes the absence from Ben Sira of mention of several important aspects of orthodox Judaism, such as the dietary laws and the proscription of images; and he observes that the Greeks are missing from the list of detested peoples in 50:26.

endorsement of Judaic tradition and in view of his explicit statement about his own method, that he intended to learn from a variety of sources and authors (39:1–2). In taking this position, Ben Sira is firmly fixed in the Judaic proverbial wisdom tradition, which maintained an internationalistic posture toward the quest for truth. The sages were the scientists of their day, and truth is unrestricted by international boundaries. To conclude, therefore, merely from the *presence* of quotations from Hellenic authors in Ben Sira, that he consciously sought to effect a fusion between Judaic and Hellenic thought would be unwarranted.

A majority of the evidence Middendorp cites in support of his "fusion" theory, of course, is in the category of those sayings which *could* have been inspired simply by Ben Sira's Judaic tradition, but which *might also* coincide with something written by a Hellenic writer. I believe that I have shown above that a careful analysis of such passages in Ben Sira will remove such confusion and will show where Ben Sira has followed Judaic tradition and where Hellenic insight. An example of a passage where clarity can be derived by such careful analysis is Sir 27:22–24,[132] where we saw that Ben Sira relies heavily—not, as Middendorp claims, on Theognis—but rather on Prov 6:12–19; yet we also saw that he may rely on Theognis in v 23, where he refers to the one who speaks well to one but ill of one when absent. What does Ben Sira think that he is doing in such an instance? Is he attempting to cite together Judaic and Hellenic material in such a way that his readers would conclude that the two were very similar? If so, why did he not quote Theognis more directly instead of so paraphrastically,[133] and what would he then expect his readers to conclude when they read so heavily Judaic a passage as 44:1–50:24? Surely a better understanding of Ben Sira's use of Hellenic material is that, when it suits his (Judaic) purpose, i.e., when he regards it as true, *he claims it for Judaism.* This is what the Jewish sages had always done, and what Ben Sira, if I may repeat this point yet again, has told us in 39:1–2 that he was doing: behaving as one "who searcheth out the wisdom of all the ancients, . . . Who heedeth the discourses of men of renown."

Having established that point, we are now in a position to make a brief statement regarding the issue of *Ben Sira and Hellenism.* While some scholars, such as Middendorp and Pautrel, see Ben Sira consciously attempting to fuse Hellenic thought with Judaism, others agree with the view of Rudolf Smend that Ben Sira announces a "declaration of war against Hellenism."[134] Thus Hengel discusses "Ben Sira's controversy

---

[132] Cf. above, pp. 33–34.

[133] Cf. again the passages in question juxtaposed above, pp. 33–34.

[134] Smend, *Weisheit*, XXIII. Also Spicq, "Ecclésiastique," 553. Smend refers especially to the opening section of Ben Sira. Smend also thought, of course, (p. XXIV), that "indeed

with Hellenistic liberalism,"[135] and E. P. Sanders refers to Sir 36:1–17 as an example of Ben Sira's "strikingly nationalistic and traditionally Jewish" attitude toward the Gentiles.[136] Robert H. Pfeiffer, also, considers one of the main purposes of Ben Sira to be "to counteract the inclination of Jerusalem's upper classes to adopt the rapidly spreading Hellenistic civilization."[137] Both Pfeiffer and Hengel note the "occasional" presence in Ben Sira of allusions to or recollections of Hellenic writings,[138] but they emphatically deny that he *endorsed* any Hellenic ideas.[139] Now, while our analysis of the alleged parallels presented by Middendorp has confirmed that position to the extent that we were able to see that Ben Sira normally takes over Hellenic material in support of a traditional Judaic position, we also saw that he is able simply to agree with a sage observation (for example, the Homeric comparison of human life to leaves on a tree, or Theognis's observation that doing a kindness to an evil person is not a good deed).[140] Thus, it is not that Ben Sira opposes Hellenic ideas *as such*, and he is even able, apparently, to read and use at least one Hellenic writer (Theognis); rather, he is entirely open to Hellenic thought *as long as it can be Judaized*.[141] What he opposes is the *dismantling of Judaism*, and this is what Smend, Pfeiffer, Hengel, and others have seen. Actually, Ben Sira does not express even this view directly, although it may be inferred from his identification of Torah with wisdom, from his statement in chap. 24 that Wisdom found a dwelling in Israel, and from his hope, expressed in 36:1–10, that Israel will be the instrument of the salvation of the world. Both Pfeiffer and Hengel cite 41:8–9 as a clear statement of opposition to Hellenism,[142] yet even there an opposition to any specific position or philosophy has to be inferred, since Ben Sira only pronounces a woe on those who have forsaken the Law. Since we, so the inference seems to run, know what

---

nothing of Greek influence in him is to be discovered." There is, quite naturally, a middle position; e.g., Lévi, *Ecclésiastique* 2. LXVI: Ben Sira is the oldest example of "l'action de l'hellénisme sur le judaisme." This last position was also that of Edersheim, "Ecclesiasticus," 19, who nevertheless expressed considerable scepticism about Ben Sira's borrowing from any other writers.

[135] Hengel, *Judaism and Hellenism*, 1. 138–53.

[136] E. P. Sanders, *Paul*, 331.

[137] Pfeiffer, *History*, 370.

[138] Ibid., 371. Hengel, as noted above (p. 55), thinks of "transmigration . . . by word of mouth."

[139] Pfeiffer, *History*, 371: "no influence of Hellenism"; Hengel, *Judaism and Hellenism*, 1. 138–39, refers to Ben Sira's identification of Torah with wisdom as proof of his particularism.

[140] Above, pp. 39, 32.

[141] So also precisely Crenshaw, *Wisdom*, 159. Crenshaw sees the threat not in assimilation—which would produce the "war" on Hellenism, but in a theological crisis, "an inability to believe in God's justice" (ibid., 172).

[142] Pfeiffer, *History*, 371; Hengel, *Judaism and Hellenism*, 1. 151.

was going on in Jerusalem in Ben Sira's day, we know where those who have forsaken the Law were going: to Hellenism.

It would appear that Ben Sira was indifferent to the issue of Hellenistic provenance of ideas. Like the sages before him, he was open to taking over a good idea from any source, as long as he could agree with it. Since he had identified the Torah with wisdom, of course he would not make use of a foreign statement or position that he considered to be in conflict with the Torah or with sagacity. What he opposed was forsaking the Law, and he was capable of being quite particularistic on occasion (50:25–26, where, as Pautrel emphasized, Greeks are not mentioned). Yet, on one occasion, he was even capable of repeating the cardinal Hellenic virtue of "moderation," just as long as he could bring it within the context of his ethics of caution (31:27).

The way in which Ben Sira used Hellenic material has occupied us at such length because we needed to have clearly in mind how he used non-Judaic writings, so that we could be in a position better to evaluate the suggestion that he also made use of Egyptian writings. It is to the possibility of such use that we now turn.

CHAPTER 3

BEN SIRA'S RELATION TO EGYPTIAN TRADITION

Egyptian Texts Other Than Papyrus Insinger

The purpose of the foregoing analysis has been to gain clarity about Ben Sira's method and procedure in his use of traditional Judaic and of foreign (Hellenic) gnomic material in order to prepare the way for an evaluation of certain Egyptian parallels to his work. We have found him to be thoroughly Jewish,[1] and we have seen that, even when he departs from the proverbial tradition or advances innovations within it, he normally relies on the Torah or on some other aspect of "the Law and the Prophets," or of the wisdom tradition. His own positions are seen in the way in which he emphasizes aspects of Judaic tradition (Torah=wisdom, caution). Foreign (Hellenic) material is clearly *supplementary*; Ben Sira uses it to support one of his Judaic positions, or simply as the raw material of scientific observation. We have thus attained a sufficient background to allow an evaluation of Egyptian parallels to Ben Sira in general and of *Papyrus Insinger* in particular.

The relation of Israelite and Jewish wisdom literature to Egyptian wisdom literature was admirably evaluated in 1929 by the Swiss scholar Paul Humbert in his *Recherches sur les sources égyptiennes de la littérature sapientiale d'Israël*.[2] For Ben Sira, Humbert was able to point, in addition to noting his "profound Jewishness,"[3] to a number of Egyptian parallels, especially from *Papyrus Insinger*. Since it is this latter category that I want especially to consider, it will be prudent to examine Humbert's other Egyptian parallels first.

The first and most obvious use of traditional Egyptian material by Ben Sira which Humbert discussed is the "satire of occupations," Sir 38:24–39:11. Ben Sira begins this section by affirming that "the wisdom of the scribe *cometh by opportunity of leisure*,[4] And he that hath little

---

[1] As P. Humbert observed (in the work cited in the following note, p. 132), "Jewish before all."

[2] (Mémoires de l'Université de Neuchatel 7; Neuchatel: Secrétariat de l'Université, 1929).

[3] Ibid., 132.

[4] The obvious synonymous parallelism of the verse seems to demand that the Greek, *en eukairiq scholēs*, must be more original.

business can become wise"; after which he satirizes the occupations, respectively, of the "fellah" (38:25–26),[5] the engraver (v 27), the smith (v 28), and the potter (v 29–30). Verses 31–34 make a general statement about the inferior position in society accorded such people, and then Ben Sira contrasts, in 39:1–11, the superior position and rewards of the scribe. Humbert noted the presence of just such a discourse in *"The Instruction of Duauf,"*[6] in which the author advised that "the scribe, his is every place at the Residence and he is not poor in it. . . . Would that I might make thee love books more than thy mother," after which he contrasted to the scribe the sculptor, the goldsmith, the artisan, the stonemason, and others.[7] Similar sections are to be found in *Papyrus Lansing,*[8] in *Papyrus Sallier* I,[9] and in *Papyrus Anastasi* V.[10]

Humbert also noted, further, that the similarities between Ben Sira and *Duauf* in their respective parallel texts extend to details, even to the choice of words.[11] Thus, of the four occupations mentioned by Ben Sira, two—engraver and smith—are specifically mentioned in *Duauf*, and the cowherd of Sir 38:25, who is also mentioned in *Papyri Lansing, Anastasi* V, and *Sallier* I, finds a reminiscence in *Duauf*'s mention of the "small bricklayer" who works "among the cattle . . . *and* swine." Again, Ben Sira's "he that hath little business" (38:24) as a description of the scribe is like *Duauf* 1, which refers to "him that is set free from forced labour"; and for the smith to sit "by the furnace" (Sir 38:28)[12] recalls the similar image in *Duauf* 3, where the smith sits "at the mouth of his furnace." Moreover, of this same smith Ben Sira says that "the flame of the fire cracketh his flesh," just as *Duauf* finds the fingers of the smith "like stuff from crocodiles."

That the engraver of Sir 38:27 works "by night as by day" is like *Duauf* 4, where the engraver, "in the night, when he is set free, . . . worketh beyond what his arms can do; in the night he burneth a light." Even Ben Sira's ideal scribe, who "searcheth out the wisdom of all the

---

5 Cf. Humbert, *Sources égyptiennes*, 126.

6 ET in A. Erman, *The Ancient Egyptians. A Sourcebook of Their Writings* (New York: Harper & Row, 1966) 67–72.

7 As Humbert pointed out (*Sources égyptiennes*, 125), he was not the first to note this similarity. It is my intention to deal with the evidence in Humbert in the same way as the evidence in Middendorp and not to refer to the earlier studies on which Humbert relies. Those studies can be found properly cited in his work. His was the first comprehensive treatment of the subject.

8 Humbert, *Sources égyptiennes*, 128–29.

9 Ibid., 129–30.

10 Ibid., 131.

11 The following list of similarities between Ben Sira and *Duauf* follows Humbert, *Sources égyptiennes*, 130–32.

12 Humbert gives "before his furnace"; both he and Box and Oesterley are reading the Syriac, *'l kwr*; "his" is, of course, correct.

ancients" (39:1), is comparable to *Duauf*'s ideal scribe, who "knoweth the books" (*Duauf* 21). Furthermore, when Ben Sira affirms that the artisans and craftsmen "shall not be inquired of for public counsel, And in the assembly they enjoy no precedence" (38:33), this is the negative version of *Duauf*'s quotation of the *Kemit* in *Duauf* 1: "The scribe, his is every place at the Residence and he is not poor in it." Finally, both *Duauf* and Ben Sira close their "satires of occupations" with firm affirmations of the "primacy" of the occupation of the scribe. In *Duauf* 20 we read, "Behold, there is no calling that is without a director except (that of) the scribe, and he is the director"; and Ben Sira's "panegyric" of 39:1–11 concludes (vv 9–11):

> His understanding many do praise,
>   And never shall his name be blotted out:[13]
> His memory shall not cease,
>   And his name shall live from generation to generation.
> His wisdom doth the congregation tell forth,
>   And his praise the assembly publisheth.
> If he live long, he shall *leave a name* more than a thousand;
>   And *if* he cometh to an end, *it* sufficeth *for him*.

Humbert did not go so far as to propose that Ben Sira had actually read *Duauf*, although he could hardly have been faulted had he done so. Rather, he stated that "the dependence of Sir 38:24–39:11 with regard to the Egyptian prototypes is evident even to the details." The problem in attempting to establish direct dependency is, of course, the state of preservation of ancient Egyptian gnomic literature; what is known today is still really only bits and scraps, and insight was passed on from one work to another, just as within the Judaic wisdom tradition; witness the aforementioned quotation of "*Kemit*" at the first of *Duauf*. Thus, even when the "dependence" of Ben Sira upon Egyptian tradition is seen "even to the details," it is not possible to say that he read *that* work, but only that he had read *a* or *some* documents having at least virtually the same content as *Duauf*.[14]

Humbert considered this parallel to be the only case of certain dependency upon Egyptian tradition in Ben Sira,[15] but he was able to cite other parallels for which he considered such dependency possible. Several lines from the tomb of Petosiris fall into this category.[16] Thus Sir 1:12, "The fear of the Lord . . . giveth . . . length of days," recalls

---

[13] The Greek has omitted "his name," which is found in the Syriac.

[14] Cf. also R. J. Williams, "The Sages of Ancient Egypt in the Light of Recent Scholarship," *JAOS* 101 (1981) 10, who refers to the influence on Sir 38:24–39:11 of the "genre" of Egyptian literature extolling the occupation of the sage.

[15] Humbert, *Sources égyptiennes*, 132.

[16] Ibid., 132–33.

Petosiris inscription 62, line 2, "He who keeps steadfastly on the path of God, his existence on earth is established" (after the French); yet Humbert noted correctly that Prov 10:27, "The fear of Yahweh prolongs *days*," seems a more likely candidate for the source of Ben Sira's statement. Closer is Petosiris 58, line 21, and 31, line 92, "Faithful to his God unto the state of being *imȝḥw*" (after the French; *imȝḥw* meaning "venerable" as applied to the aged and the dead) to Sir 1:13: "Whoso feareth the Lord, it shall go well with him at the last, And in the day of his death he shall be blessed," where Ben Sira's "blessing" corresponds exactly, according to Humbert, to Petosiris's "veneration." The nearest Judaic parallel to this verse which Humbert could cite was Prov 10:7, "The memory of the righteous is a blessing," which he considered not quite "*étroit*." One should also, however, recall the frequent admonitions in the historical prologue to the Central Discourse of Deuteronomy to the effect that Israel should love or fear Yahweh, e.g., Deut 6:2," . . . that you may fear Yahweh your God," and 6:5, "You shall love Yahweh your God," in the context of which one finds the promise of 7:14: "You shall be blessed above all peoples." In Sir 1:13, of course, this Deuteronomic righteousness has been applied in a personal way and related to the blessed or venerable conclusion of the life of the individual righteous one. This is probably, indeed, an Egyptian trait, although likely not directly dependent on inscriptions from the tomb of Petosiris. The theme will engage us again further below.

Humbert also observed that inscriptions from the tomb of Petosiris referred to the fear of God of the departed righteous, but he quite naturally and correctly then recalled the preponderance of this theme in the Bible.

Humbert found a parallel between *Ptahhotep* 30, "Do not rely on thy wealth, which has been granted to thee as a gift from God" (after Humbert's French), and Sir 5:1, which he rendered, "Do not trust in thy wealth, and do not say, 'I have the means!'"[17] (similarly Box and Oesterley, *APOT* 1). Yet one should also note Ps 62:10: "If riches increase, set not your heart on them." Reliance on *Ptahhotep* is thus doubtful here.

Humbert also found a parallel between Ben Sira's discussion of caution in friendship, Sir 6:5–17, and statements in *Ptahhotep* and *Papyrus Insinger*.[18] He noted that *Papyrus Insinger* develops this theme "at length" (*PIns.* xi23–xii18) and concludes (xii18) by observing, "One does not get to know the heart of a companion if one has not asked him for advice in need." Yet Humbert observed that one finds already in *Ptahhotep* 33, "If thou lookest for a state of friendhsip, ask no question, but draw near him and be with him alone. . . . Prove (?) his heart by a

---

17 Ibid., 133–34.
18 Ibid., 134.

conversation," which he found to be quite close to Sir 6:7, "If thou *acquirest* a friend *acquire him by testing*, And be not in haste to trust him." We have already seen that Ben Sira seems to rely on Theognis in this section,[19] and we also saw that Sir 6:7 is rather like a line from Xenophon.[20] All the parallels to Theognis here fall between Sir 6:10 and 16, however, leaving one to inquire whether Ben Sira has, in 6:7, relied on Xenophon or on Egyptian material, or whether the parallel is merely coincidental. We reserve judgment on this suggested parallel for the present and will return to it below in the discussion of *Papyrus Insinger*.

Humbert's suggestion that the repeated parallelism in Sir 7:4–5 between God and king reflects Egyptian notions of divine kingship is something of a long shot.[21] It would have been impossible for Ben Sira consciously to have intended this parallelism to be synonymous, since the Davidic monarchy—where would have existed for Ben Sira the only possible candidate for such a divine king—had long since ceased to exist, and Ben Sira could not have intended a *non*-Jewish king as divine! Did Ben Sira then simply take over this phrasing, originally meant synonymously, and redirect it as synthetic parallelism (as it now stands)? This is possible, but one would have to see a more exact formulation in order to be certain. The statements about God and king in Sir 7:4–5, in other words, could readily have occurred to Ben Sira without his thinking of Egyptian ideas of divine kingship.

Sir 7:27–28 contains an expansion on the fifth commandment,[22] noting especially the birth pangs of the mother (v 27b) and concluding, "How canst thou recompense them for what they have done for thee?" Just these non-biblical traits are found in *Ani* 37 regarding one's mother: "Double the bread that thou givest to thy mother, and carry her as she carried (thee). She had a heavy load in thee. . . . When thou wast born after thy months, she carried thee yet again about her neck," etc.[23] A connection appears to be possible. Humbert's noting, however, a parallel between Sir 7:32, "Also to the poor stretch out thy hand, That *thy* blessing may be perfected," and *Ani* 38, "Eat not bread, if another is suffering want, and thou dost not stretch out the hand to him with bread,"[24] loses significance when one recalls the prevalence of the virtue of

---

[19] Above, pp. 30–31.

[20] Above, p. 44.

[21] Humbert, *Sources égyptiennes*, 134.

[22] These verses do not appear in the Hebrew text, but their presence in both the Greek and the Syriac and the possibility of haplography (*bkl lbk* at the beginning of 27 and 29) make it likely that they are original. Cf. Box and Oesterley, *APOT* 1. Also Duesberg et Auvray, *Ecclésiastique*, Spicq, "Ecclésiastique," Peters, *Jesus Sirach*, and Smend, *Weisheit*. Lévi, *Ecclésiastique* 2, rejects them.

[23] Humbert, *Sources égyptiennes*, 134–35.

[24] Ibid., 135.

almsgiving in the Ancient Near East,[25] and when one notes that the key word, "blessing," absent in the version of the saying in *Ani*, appears in Prov 22:9: "He who has a bountiful eye will be blessed, for he shares his bread with the poor."

Humbert suggested that Sir 7:33b, "From the dead withhold not kindness (*ḥsd*)," represents an acceptance of the Egyptian custom of offerings to the dead. Such a connection would appear to be possible, although Ben Sira is too indefinite here for one to be certain what he has in mind. Deut 26:14 appears to make grave offerings illegal or at least improper, and such seems not to have been ancient Judaic practice.[26]

As parallel to Sir 19:7, "Never repeat a word,—Then no one will reproach thee,"[27] Humbert suggests *Ani* 33, "A wrong word that hath come forth from thy mouth, if (he?) repeateth it, thou makest enemies (for thyself)." One may also cite Prov 17:9: "He who repeats a matter alienates a friend"; yet, it would appear that *Ani*'s "animosity" is nearer Ben Sira's "reproach" than is the "alienation" (*maprîd*) of Proverbs. All three forms of the proverb are sufficiently similar, however, that one would hesitate to assume dependence of any one on the other. We probably have to do here with a universal bit of practical advice.

Humbert also notes Egyptian parallels for Sir 31:12–32:13, the section on banqueting and drinking advice. We saw above,[28] in the discussion of Theognis parallels, that this section of Ben Sira contains several close parallels to statements of Theognis regarding *caution in drinking*, so as to lead one to the conclusion that Ben Sira had relied on Theognis here in his drinking advice. The passage as a whole, however, bears overwhelmingly Egyptian traits. Humbert cites 31:12–13a, 14, 16a, d, 18–19a:

> *My son*, if thou sittest at a great man's table,
>   Be not greedy upon it;
> Say not: There is abundance upon it—
>   Remember that an evil eye is an evil thing,
>
> . . . .
>
> Stretch not out the hand wherever he may look,
>   And collide not with him in the dish.
>
> . . . .
>
> *Take thy seat like a man that is chosen,*
>
> . . . .
>
> *And be not gluttonous, lest thou be rejected.*
>
> . . . .

---

[25] Cf. above, p. 8.

[26] Cf. the discussion in G. F. Moore, *Judaism in the First Centuries of the Christian Era* (New York: Schocken, 1971), 2. 288.

[27] Humbert, *Sources égyptiennes*, 136. Humbert here follows the Syriac for the second stich of the line, as do Box and Oesterley, *APOT* 1. So also Segal, *Spr Bn Syr'*.

[28] Above, pp. 34–35.

And, moreover, when thou art seated in a large company
Stretch not the hand out before a neighbour.
Surely a little is sufficient for a man of understanding.[29]

Advice of this kind is widespread in Egyptian gnomic literature, and Humbert cites especially *Ptahhotep* 7:

If thou art one of those sitting at the table of one greater than thyself, take what he may give, when it is set before thy nose. Thou shouldst gaze at what is before thee. Do not pierce him with many stares;

and *Kagemni* 2 and 3:[30]

If thou sittest with many persons, hold the food in abhorrence, even if thou desirest it; it taketh only a brief moment to master oneself, and it is disgraceful to be greedy.

. . . .

If thou sittest with a greedy person, eat thou only when his meal is over, and if thou sittest with a drunkard, take thou only when his desire is satisfied. Rage not against the meat in the presence of a . . . ; take when he giveth thee, and refuse it not.

Surely here, as clearly as was the case with the "satire of occupations," Ben Sira has taken up characteristic Egyptian advice, although this particular Egyptian theme was likely derived from the version of *Amene-mope* that appears in Prov 23:1–3,

When you sit down to eat with a ruler,
     observe carefully what is before you;
and put a knife to your throat
     if you are a man given to appetite.
Do not desire his delicacies,
     for they are deceptive food.

One will note the similarity in order between this chain of proverbs and Sir 31:12, 13a, 14.[31]

Humbert thinks that one can see Ben Sira, in Sir 40:1–10, taking up the traditional Egyptian theme of human misery and modifying it in terms of his more optimistic view of the punishment of the wicked (only). Ben Sira begins this section by writing, in part,

Much occupation hath God apportioned,
     And heavy is the *injustice* upon the sons of men—

---

[29] Humbert, *Sources égyptiennes*, 137.
[30] Ibid., 137–38.
[31] The motif appears not to be Hellenic. The parallels cited by Middendorp, *Stellung*, 23, are irrelevant for Ben Sira's code of banqueting ethics. Hengel, *Judaism and Hellenism*, 1. 150, assumes the influence of "Greek conventions" but cites no Hellenic parallels. Middendorp, *Stellung*, 82, also refers to Prov 23:1–3.

From the day that he cometh forth from his mother's womb,
  Until the day when he returneth to the mother of all living:
From him that sitteth in exaltation on a throne,
  Unto him that *sitteth in*[32] dust and ashes;

. . . .

Surely jealousy, anxiety and fear,
  Terror of death, strife,[33] and contention!
                (Sir 40:1, 3, 5a)[34]

Verses 9–10, then—and already v 8b, if the Greek has reproduced the
missing Hebrew accurately—refer only to the wicked. Thus v 10 states,
"For the wicked evil is created"; and this Humbert takes to be Ben Sira's
alteration of the statement in vv 1–8a of general human misery, which
has many Egyptian ancestors. Without quoting any Egyptian texts,
Humbert refers to the "Dialogue of the One Tired of Life," as well as to
several other Egyptian works.[35] The connection appears likely. All the
remaining Egyptian parallels to Ben Sira cited by Humbert are from
Papyrus Insinger, and these will be considered presently, after an
examination of a further parallel alleged by another scholar.

  Siegfried Morenz has conjectured the possible influence of Egyptian
wisdom on Ben Sira in Sir 33:13–15, where the image of God the potter
who makes both the good and the evil is reminiscent of *Amenemope*
24.13.7, "Man is clay and straw, And the god is his builder. He is tearing
down and building up every day. He makes a thousand poor men as he
wishes, (Or) he makes a thousand men *as overseers*."[36] Morenz argues
that the qualitative difference expressed in these two places (as well as in
Wis 15:7 and Rom 9:21) between human beings and the god who can
make them as he will is not a traditionally Judaic concept but comes into
Hellenistic Judaism, and thence into Christianity, from the Egyptian
idea expressed by *Amenemope*. I have the impression, however, that the

---

[32] The text reads *'d lšwb 'pr w'pr* with a marginal reading for *lšwb* of *lbš, lwbš*, for which
Box and Oesterley, *APOT* 1, read *lĕbûš* and translate, "is clothed with," also Peters, *Jesus
Sirach*; yet this phrase still requires a *b* understood before *'pr*. More likely, the Syriac—as
Smend, *Weisheit*, 369 suggested—which has *ytb* in both stichoi of the verse (the Hebrew has
yšb in the first stichos, parallel to the disputed word in the second stichos), is correct, and the
text originally read . . . *'d lywšb b'pr*, which was then corrupted to the present text of MS B.
Duesberg et Auvray, *Ecclésiastique*, read "*siège . . . assis*" and Spicq, "Ecclésiastique,"
"*assis . . . accroupi*" and thus apparently also prefer the Syriac reading. Lévi, *Ecclésiastique*
2, translates, "*siège . . . accroupi*," but does not emend the text. Ryssel, "Jesus Sirach,"
argued for the superiority of the Greek. Smend, *Weisheit*, also noted that in v 4, which
extends the parallelism of v 3, the same verb (*'th*) is used in both stichoi.

[33] The emendation from *hrh* to *hrh* must surely be correct. So all the commentators.

[34] Verse 2, missing in the Hebrew, is omitted here.

[35] Humbert, *Sources égyptiennes*, 143.

[36] S. Morenz, "Eine weitere Spur der Weisheit Amenopes in der Bibel," *Zeitschrift für
ägyptische Sprache und Altertumskunde* 84 (1959) 79–80.

figure of the potter in Jeremiah 18, in which God declares his right to support or to destroy a nation, is a specific application of a more general figure. If that is the case, then Ben Sira could be relying in 33:13–15 on a traditional Judaic image, which just happens not to appear in any surviving Judaic literature written prior to his time. But the matter remains uncertain.

All the remaining Egyptian parallels to Ben Sira cited by Humbert are from *Papyrus Insinger*. Since it is the work of which this papyrus is an exemplar that will occupy our attention from this point on, we should summarize briefly the extent and the nature of the Egyptian parallels to Ben Sira from other sources.

That the "satire of occupations" in 38:24–39:11 relies on an Egyptian antecedent seems beyond doubt. Here Ben Sira has taken over, lock-stock-barrel, both the content and the point of view of an Egyptian text, and this borrowing is more obvious and his reliance on foreign tradition more pronounced than was the case with any of the Hellenic gnomic materials. While the Egyptian material used here falls under the already defined category of use of sage observation with which Ben Sira agrees,[37] still the extent of Ben Sira's reliance in this case tells us that he is perhaps more comfortable with and more apt to use Egyptian material than he is Hellenic. The same remarks could apply almost as emphatically to the section on table manners, Sir 31:12–24.[38] Here, however, the advice supports Ben Sira's ethics of caution. The other likely cases of dependency on Egyptian sources reveal Ben Sira, again as in the case of Theognis, simply citing sage observation with which he is able to agree (the blessing or veneration of the individual righteous,[39] the propriety of giving recompense to parents,[40] and the universality of human misery[41]) or employing other material which supports his ethics of caution.[42] As Humbert noted,[43] this meager evidence is hardly sufficient to convince us that Ben Sira relied very heavily on Egyptian materials. But this issue appears in a different light when *Papyrus Insinger* is examined for parallels to Ben Sira.

Phibis (Papyrus Insinger) *in Paul Humbert's Analysis*

Before we proceed with the issue: *Papyrus Insinger* and Ben Sira, it would seem appropriate to give a brief, general explanation about this

---

[37] See above, p. 56.
[38] Above, pp. 66–67.
[39] Above, pp. 63–64.
[40] Above, p. 65.
[41] Above, pp. 67–68.
[42] Above, pp. 64–65.
[43] Humbert, *Sources égyptiennes*, 132.

papyrus. The papyrus contains most of an Egyptian gnomic work in Demotic, being about three-fourths complete. The beginning is lost,[44] and the papyrus begins near the end of chapter, or "Instruction," 6 and continues through the 25th Instruction to the end, where a subscription apparently names the author as Phibis, son of Tachos-pa-iana.[45] It occupies thirty-five columns, most of the first and a good part of the second being poorly preserved; but the rest of the MS is generally well preserved. The first editor dated it, solely on the basis of about half a dozen lines of Greek of about ten letters each on the reverse of one of the columns, in the first decade of the first century C.E.; he noted that the character of the Demotic script did not argue against such a date.[46] This date was universally accepted until other Papyri—*Carlsberg Papyri* II, III verso, IV verso, and V—were discovered by Aksel Volten to contain fragments of the same work, and Volten's studies of the several papyri led him to date the original work, which he titled "*Das demotische Weisheitsbuch*," "probably" in pre-Ptolemaic times.[47] This earlier dating has now attracted further scholarly support,[48] so that it seems to be a safe assumption that the work originated somewhat before or perhaps even during Ben Sira's own time.

We saw above (p. 64) that Humbert suggested the possibility of some connection between *PIns.* xi23–xii18 and Sir 6:5–17. Some further observations regarding the indicated section of *Papyrus Insinger* may help to clarify the issue. *PIns.* xi23, "Do not trust the one whom you do not know in your heart, lest he deceitfully cheat you," may be compared to Sir 6:7b, "Be not in haste to trust" a friend; *PIns.* xii8, "Do not trust your enemy," recalls Sir 6:13b, "Separate thyself from thine enemies"; and *PIns.* xii15, "one does not get to know the heart of a smart man if one has not tested him somehow," recalls again Sir 6:7a (above). Because of this considerable agreement within similar sections, one could perhaps

---

[44] As Williams, "Sages," 2, reports, "Two large papyrus fragments" of this missing beginning have been located in the University Museum of Philadelphia. They have not, however, been published.

[45] "The end of the royal book. The soul of Phibis, son of Tachos-pa-iana, is rejuvenated for eternity. It will follow Sokar-Osiris, the great god, Lord of Abydos; his soul is rejuvenated upon his body for all eternity" (*PIns.* xxxv13–15). The ET of *Phibis* given here follows the German of F. W. Freiherr von Bissing, ed. and trans., *Altägyptische Lebensweisheit* (Zurich: Artemis, 1955) 91–120.

[46] Cf. *Monuments égyptiens du musée d'antiquités des pays-bas à Leide: Suten-χeft, le livre royal. Papyrus Démotique Insinger* (34e livraison), (transcription, with introduction by W. Pleyte and P. A. A. Boeser; Leiden: Brill, 1899) 11; and the supplement to same: *Édition en phototypie* (1905), col. I.

[47] A. Volten, *Das demotische Weisheitsbuch* (Copenhagen: Munksgaard, 1941) 123.

[48] E.g., J. Marböck, *Weisheit im Wandel. Untersuchungen zur Weisheitstheologie bei Ben Sira* (BBB 37; Bonn: Peter Hanstein, 1971) 169, who suggests, to be more precise, the third or second century B.C.E.

suggest that these lines from *Papyrus Insinger* strengthen the conjecture of an Egyptian background for Sir 6:5–9 and that *PIns*. xii8, about the enemy, forms the tie to the Theognis material, which then predominates in Sir 6:10–15.

As further Ben Sira/*Insinger* parallels, then, Humbert first cites Sir 9:2, "Give not thyself unto a woman, So as to let her trample down thy manhood,"[49] and *PIns*. viii4, "If a woman is beautiful, your lord is revealed in her,"[50] sayings which seem to have the same general meaning; yet one should also note Prov 31:3: "Give not your strength to women." A rather more striking parallel is provided by the respective sayings about the bee, "never used as term of comparison in Proverbs":[51] Sir 11:3, "Of no account among flying things is the bee, But her fruit is supreme among products," and *PIns*. xxv2: "A little bee brings the honey." Equally as noteworthy is the fact that both *Phibis* and Ben Sira mention one hundred years as the limit of life;[52] Sir 18:9: "The number of man's days *is* great (if it reach) an hundred years," and *PIns*. xvii21: "Even when life approaches one hundred years, still a fourth of it is lost."[53]

Humbert next refers to the section "against women, good living, and drunkenness" in Sir 18:30–19:3 and cites especially 19:2, "Wine and women make the heart lustful, and an *impudent* soul will destroy its owner"; and he notes the parallel section in the 8th Instruction of *Phibis*, especially *PIns*. vi1,[54] "The evil that happens to the fool, his stomach and his phallus bring (him)." Now, Ben Sira seems to have relied at this point on two proverbs from the Book of Proverbs which occur there in reasonably close proximity to each other.[55] Thus one may compare Prov 21:17, "He who loves pleasure will be a poor man; he who loves wine and oil will not be rich," with Sir 19:1, "He that doeth this [i.e., is intemperate] will not become rich," and Prov 23:20–21, "Be not among winebibbers, or among gluttonous eaters of meat; for the drunkard and the

---

[49] For the translation, cf. the notes given by Box and Oesterley, *APOT* 1.

[50] Humbert, *Sources égyptiennes*, 135.

[51] Ibid. The example, including the contrast, does appear in Prov 6:8c LXX. That the Greek translation of Proverbs has influenced Ben Sira in any way I strongly doubt; LXX has independently taken up the Egyptian saying!

[52] Ibid., 136.

[53] Isa 65:20 also refers to a life span of 100 years. While the context there is the "new heavens and a new earth," still the miraculous or utopian element is that people will not die prematurely, i.e., before 100 years of life, so that 100 years appears to be understood as the "proper" human lifespan. The occurrence of such a notion in the third Isaiah may mean that it was current in Ben Sira's day. Both Ben Sira and *Phibis*, however, are emphasizing the weakness of human existence, and both emphasize that 100 years is the upper limit of longevity.

[54] Humbert, *Sources égyptiennes*, 136.

[55] So Middendorp, *Stellung*, 81.

glutton will come to poverty," with Sir 18:32, "Delight not thyself in a *whisper of* luxury, For double is the poverty thereof." There are, nevertheless, some further reasons for thinking that there may be some connection between Sir 18:30–19:3 and the 8th Instruction of *Phibis*. One is, of course, that both Ben Sira and *Phibis* have *sections* on the destructive consequences of intemperance; and both also refer to intemperance with women (*PIns.* v22 and Sir 19:2). There is, further, a very close parallel between Ben Sira's reference to "squandering" here (18:33) and a nearby line in *Phibis* (cf. below, pp. 85–86). Thus one would have to reckon with the possibility that Ben Sira has made use of both Proverbs and *Phibis* in this short section.

Humbert next notes that both Ben Sira and *Phibis* devote considerable sections to the education of children (Sir 30:1–13 and the 10th Instruction of *Phibis*, *PIns.* viii21–ix20), and that "both recommend *l'usage pédagogique du baton.*"[56] Thus Ben Sira states in 30:1 that "he that loveth his son will continue (to lay) strokes upon him, That he may rejoice over him at the last"; and *Phibis* notes in *PIns.* ix6, following several lines dealing with the instruction of a son, "Thoth, the great god, has put the rod upon earth in order to instruct the stupid with it," and he noted in line 9 that "a son does not die from blows at the hand of the father." Ben Sira observes further, in 30:8–9,

> An unbroken horse becometh stubborn,
> And a son left at large becometh headstrong.
> Cocker thy son and he will terrify thee;
> Play with him and he will grieve thee;

and with this may be compared *PIns.* ix12–13, "A son who has not been trained, about [his father] all people wonder. His father's heart does not wish (such a one) a long life."

It is likely, however, that Ben Sira relies heavily here on Judaic proverbial tradition. Thus Prov 13:24 advises the rod,[57] and one may read in Prov 29:15, 17a, "The rod and reproof give wisdom, but a child *sent away* brings shame to his mother. . . . *Train* your son, and he will give you rest." Psalm 127:5, further, asserts regarding sons, "Happy is the man who has his quiver full of them! He shall not be put to shame when he speaks with his enemies in the gate"; cf. Sir 30:6, "Against enemies he hath left behind an avenger." What Ben Sira and *Phibis* do have in common in these sections, over against the Book of Proverbs, is that both have constructed "chapters" on the same theme.

Both Ben Sira and *Phibis*, according to Humbert, "recommend not

---

56 Humbert, *Sources égyptiennes*, 136–37.
57 Above, p. 6.

giving oneself over uselessly to care."[58] He refers to Sir 30:21ff. and 38:18ff. and cites 30:21–24:

> 21 Give not thy soul to sorrow,
>   And let not thyself become unsteadied with care.
> 22 Heart-joy is life for a man,
>   And human gladness prolongeth days.
> 23 Entice thyself and soothe thine heart,
>   And banish vexation from thee;
>   For sorrow hath slain many,
>   And there is no profit in vexation.
> 24 Envy and anger shorten days,
>   And anxiety maketh old untimely.

So also *PIns.* xix6–7: "Instruction 17. Do not abandon yourself to sorrow, lest you become restless. If the heart is concerned for its master, it engenders sickness in him."

When one examines the Hebrew text of Ben Sira, however, this parallel becomes somewhat less certain. Virtually all the commentators make conjectural emendations in the text, so that it reads as the Box and Oesterley translation given above—so also Humbert. According to this understanding, *dyn* in Sir 30:21, 23 is taken to be a "graphical mistake" for *dwn*,[59] a word related to the Syriac *dwwn'* (given in the Syriac version in both instances); thus the translation "sorrow." The Greek also gives *lypē* in these two cases. When *dyn* appears again in v 24, the Syriac and Greek give different translations, and Box and Oesterley translate "anger." Now, it must be admitted that the evidence is strong that the Syriac and Greek have read one word in vv 21 and 23 and another in v 24, for all of which we now have only the *dyn* of MS B. Yet there is nothing inherently problematical with reading *dyn* in all three instances, and the section in fact becomes more of a coherent whole if it is so read, thereby appearing to be a unified discourse on the disabling effects of "anger."

A further emendation is conjectured for the end of v 21, where the commentators and Humbert read *'ṣh* (with Bmg.) for *'wn* and translate "care" (Duesberg et Auvray, *Ecclésiastique*: "*idées noires*," Peters, *Jesus Sirach*: "*Grübeln*"). Yet here Box and Oesterley, *APOT* 1, note the similarity of the entire stich to Ps 31:10c: "My strength *stumbles* because of my iniquity." Again, both the Syriac and the Greek have read *'ṣh* (*mlk'*, *boulē*), but the parallel with Ps 31:10 makes the evidence of the translations less

---

[58] Humbert, *Sources égyptiennes*, 137.

[59] Box and Oesterley, *APOT* 1; also Smend, *Weisheit*, Peters, *Jesus Sirach*. Duesberg et Auvray, *Ecclésiastique*: "*tristesse*," Spicq, "Ecclésiastique": "*chagrin*." Lévi, *Ecclésiastique* 2, translates *dyn* as "*chagrin*"; but his citation of 14:1 as justification is insufficient support.

persuasive. Ben Sira was likely quoting the psalm here.[60] Now Ps 31:10 also begins, "My life is spent with sorrow,"[61] a fact which might lend support to the conjecture that Sir 30:21a originally referred to sorrow and not to anger; yet the psalmist wrote *ygwn*, not *dwn*, so that there is less likely support in Ps 31:10a for the reading *dwn* in Sir 30:21a.

One other conjectural emendation and a translational variant given for the passage are minor; the word *qṣpwn* in v 23d would be rendered better by "wrath" than by "vexation" (Box and Oesterley) or "care" (Humbert), and there appears to be no need to read *ymyw*[62] instead of *'pw* for the last word in v 22, since the text as it stands refers to "postponing anger" and is then quite understandable in view of the references to "anger" and "iniquity" in v 21 and to "anger" in v 23. It would thus appear that Sir 30:21–24 is an uncertain parallel to *PIns.* xix6–7. Sir 38:18–20 is better:

> 18 Out of *anger* proceedeth *mischief;*
>   Even so sadness of heart *buildeth pain.*
> 20 *Turn not thy heart back to him [sc. the deceased] again:*
>   Dismiss the remembrance of him, and remember the end.[63]

Here, again, the word *dyn* is taken by the commentators to be a mistake for *dwn*, so that Box and Oesterley translate "Out of sorrow proceedeth . . ."; yet the verse should be read as synthetic parallelism, not as synonymous: *As* (judgmental) anger has a harmful effect, so also sadness. This is the meaning of *PIns.* xix6–7; indeed, Sir 38:18b is verbally quite close to *PIns.* xix7.

As parallel to Sir 37:29–30,

> Indulge not *in every* enjoyment,
>   Nor *be immoderate about every dainty.*
> For in much *indulgence* nesteth sickness,
>   And he that *increaseth* cometh nigh to loathing,

Humbert cites *PIns.* vi12–14:[64] "Whoever satisfies himself too much with food has to go to bed with a pain. Whoever satisfies himself with too much wine has to go to bed with a hangover. Every illness in the parts (of the body) is a consequence of immoderation." If one follows the B text of Ben Sira, however, in reading *mbrh* ("increaseth"; so Vattioni

---

60 Smend, *Weisheit*, 270, takes '*wn* in Sir 30:21 to be a "mistake" that has "come in from" Ps 31:10; similarly Lévi, *Ecclésiastique* 2. 133.

61 Noted by Box and Oesterley, *APOT* 1.

62 Box and Oesterley, *APOT* 1; Lévi, *Ecclésiastique* 2; Duesberg et Auvray, *Ecclésiastique:* "days"; Smend, *Weisheit, ymym.* Peters, *Jesus Sirach,* however, correctly.

63 Verse 19 does not appear in the Hebrew.

64 Humbert, *Sources égyptiennes,* 138.

and above) instead of *mzy'* ("he whose stomach rumbles")[65] with MS D
and Bmg. (so Humbert), it is possible to find other parallels with *Phibis*,
since the loathsomeness of the big-bellied person is also a theme there.
Thus *PIns*. xxvi17 observes that "whoever controls himself in his sustenance of life is not despised because of his belly"; cf. also xxv18: "Love
not your belly."

Humbert quotes at some length Ben Sira's discussion of the physician
in 38:1–15:[66]

> 1 Cultivate the physician in accordance with the need of him,
>   For him also hath God ordained.
> 2 It is from God that the physician getteth wisdom,
>   And from the king he receiveth gifts.
> 3 The *physician's knowledge* lifteth up his head,
>   And he may stand before nobles.
> 4 God hath *brought forth* medicines out of the earth,
>   And let not a discerning man reject them.
>
> . . . .
>
> 7 By means of them the physician assuageth pain.
>
> . . . .
>
> 14   For he also maketh supplication to God,
>   To make *successful* his diagnosis,
>   And the *medicine (given) for the sake of sustenance*.
> 15 He that sinneth before his Maker
>   *Is presumptuous before* the physician.

He notes that this may be a conscious contrast to the viewpoint expressed
by the Chronicler in 2 Chr 16:12, where king Asa is reproached for having
resorted to physicians and not to God when ill; but he states that "it seems
natural enough to attribute this amplitude on the part of an author who has
otherwise known Egypt to the great role which medicine played in Egypt
since its origins"; and he cites especially *PIns*. xxxii12: "He (God) has
created medicine in order to remove illness"; and xxiv2: "Do not regard a
minor illness as too insignificant for medicine. Use medicine." While these
lines from *Phibis* correspond exactly to Sir 38:4a and b, one does not find
the praise of the physician in the Demotic work; so that, whereas Sir 38:4
may rely on *Phibis*, it is also conceivable that the entire section relies on
another Egyptian text, as yet unknown to moderns.[67]

Humbert next refers to the "two hymns in honor of creation and of the
Creator" in Ben Sira, 39:12–35 and 42:15–43:33,[68] and, as a parallel text in
Phibis, he quotes the entire 24th Instruction (xxx18–xxxiii6),[69] which is

---

[65] This is the best that I can do with a "strengthened qal" of "to tremble."

[66] Humbert, *Sources égyptiennes*, 138–39.

[67] Sir 38:5, further, alludes obviously to Exod 15:23–25; cf. Middendorp, *Stellung*, 59.

[68] Humbert, *Sources égyptiennes*, 140.

[69] Ibid., 140–41.

entitled, "The way to recognize the greatness of God, in order to cause it to exist in your heart." What is similar and what different may best be seen if parts of both texts are reproduced here at some length.

> [The works of] God are all good,
> > And *he supplies* every need in its season.
> *And what wilt thou compare . . . ?*
> > And the utterance of His mouth *is a* treasur*e*.
> In His place His good pleasure *maketh prosperous,*
> > And there is no restraint to His deliverance.
> The works of all flesh are before Him,
> > And there is nothing hid from before His eyes.
> From everlasting to everlasting He beholdeth;
> > [Is] there limit to His deliverance?
> There is nothing *insignificant* or *small* with Him;
> > *And* there is nothing too *difficult* or hard for Him.
> None may say: Wherefore is this?
> > For everything is selected for its *need.*
> None may say: This is worse than that;
> > For everything availeth in its season.
> His blessing overfloweth as the Nile,
> > And saturateth the world like the River.
> Even so His wrath dispossesseth nations,
> > And He turneth a watered land into salt.
> . . . .[70]
> [Good things for the g]ood hath He allotted from the beginning;
> > Even so to the evil good and evil.
> (The chief of all the necessaries) of life for man
> > Are water and fire, and iron and salt,
> The fat of wheat, milk and honey,
> > The blood of the grape, oil and clothing.
> All these prove good to the good—
> > Even so for the evil they are turned to evil.
> There are (winds) which are formed (for *judgement*),
> > (And in their fury) remove moun(tains).
> [In the season of *arrogance one sees* their *strength,*
> > And *they quiet* the *anger* of their creator.]
> Fire and hail, *evil* and pestilence—
> > These also are formed for judgement.
> Beas*t* of prey, scorpion and vipe*r,*
> > And the avenging sword to exterminate the wicked—
> All these are created for their uses,
> > And are in the treasure-house, *and at the (right) time they are appointed:*

---

[70] None of the interpretations proposed for the apparently corrupt v 24 by various commentators seems to make any sense in the context, and I therefore omit it as a verse that apparently has been placed in this position mistakenly and then misunderstood.

When he giveth them the command they rejoice,
> And in their prescribed tasks disobey not His behest.

> > (Sir 39:16–31)

I would fain remember God's works,
> And what I have seen I would recount.

In a saying of God is his good pleasure,
> And what was wrought by His good pleasure *is his teaching.*

The rising sun is revealed over all things,
> And the glory of Yahweh is over all His works.

God's holy ones have not the power
> To recount *the* wondrous works of *Yahweh*;

(Though) God hath given strength to His hosts
> To endure in the presence of His glory.

He searcheth out the deep and (man's) heart,
> And *considereth diligently all their nakedness*:

For *the Most High* possesseth knowledge . . . ,
> And *payeth attention to* what cometh *eternally.*

. . . .

The sun *bursting forth in its enclosure of heat—*
> How awe-inspiring *are* the works of Yahweh!

At noontide he bringeth the world to boiling heat,
> And before his scorching heat who can maintain himself?

(*As*) a *blown* furnace (*bringeth*) *a molten support from them,*
> (So) the sun's dart setteth the mountains ablaze:

A tongue of flame *bringeth to an end* the inhabited (world),
> And with its fire the eye is scorched.

For great is Yahweh that made him,
> And His words make His mighty *ones to be in charge.*

Moreover, the *monthly* moon *for seasonal times,*
> To rule over periods for an everlasting sign:

In them the feasts and times *are* prescribed,
> And he [*make*]*th delight by his circuit:*

Month by month *he* reneweth *himself—*
> How *awe-inspiring* is *he* in *his* changing!

. . . .

A healing for all is *dew dropping from* the clouds,
> *A releaser to make fat the parched earth.*

From His counsel He hath *made an arsenal of much,*
> And hath planted the islands in the ocean.

They that go down to the sea tell of its extent,
> And when our ears hear it we are astonished.

Therein are marvels, the most wondrous of His works,
> All kinds of living things, and the monsters *in great number.*

By reason of Him *a messenger rusheth,*
> And *by* His words *He worketh His good pleasure.*

> > (Sir 42:15–18; 43:2–8, 22–26)

24th Instruction

> The way to recognize the greatness of God, in order to cause it to
>   exist in your heart.
>
> .   .   .   .
>
> Heart and tongue without sin bring reward.
> The work of God is only a joke for the heart of the fool.
> The life of the fool is a burden to God.
> Lifetime is granted to the fool in order to allow him to live with
>   retribution.
>
> .   .   .   .
>
> A godless one does not say, God is in the arrangement of things
>   which he commands.
> Whoever says, It is not, might observe the hidden.
> How do sun and moon travel in heaven?
> Whither go water and fire and wind?
> For whom do talismans and knots become medicine?
> God makes his hidden work known on earth daily;
> he causes light and darkness to exist, in which every creature is
>   secure.
> He causes the earth to bear millions, to swallow up, and to bear again.
> He causes day, month, year to exist according to the commands of
>   the lord of commandments.
> He causes summer and winter to exist by the rising and setting of
>   Sirius.
> He causes food for the living to happen, the miracle of the field.
> He causes the constellations to exist in heaven; those who dwell on
>   earth observe them.
> He causes sweet water, which all lands wish, to exist on earth.
> He causes the breath of life to originate in eggs without there having
>   been any guidance present.
>
> .   .   .   .
>
> He causes stones and bones to happen,
> creates the coming and going of the whole earth along with the
>   movement of the ground.
> He has created sleep in order to remove tiredness, the dream in
>   order to remove the struggle for livelihood.
> He has created medicine in order to remove illness, wine in order to
>   remove depression.
> He has created the dream in order to direct its blind master.
> He causes death and life to exist before him,
> the blessing of justice and the curse of injustice.
> He causes the work of the fool for many to become food.
> He causes one after the other to happen in the species that allows
>   them to continue living.
> He gives his commandment to those who dwell on earth but hides
>   himself from them, so that they do not know him.
>
> .   .   .   .

Fate and retribution cause that which he commands to happen and
   to occur.
Fate does not look ahead of itself, retribution does not come and go
   forcefully.
The counsel of God puts one after the other.

                    (*PIns*. xxx17–23; xxxi18–xxxii18; xxxiii3–5)

Humbert is reminded by the two hymns in Ben Sira of "analogous
hymns" in Job, as well as of "numerous prototypes" in Egyptian literature; but he thinks that *Phibis* is sufficiently similar to Ben Sira here that
one may perhaps conclude that Ben Sira's insertion of these hymns is an
imitation of a style that he has observed "in the literature of Ptolemaic
scribes."[71] Humbert further notes that such hymns sometimes belong
under the category of "demonstration of the 'mysteries' of God." Thus he
cites *PIns*. xxxi9, "Whoever says, It is not (regarding God's providential
acts under discussion), might observe the hidden"; Job 38:2 + 42:5, "Who
is this that darkens counsel by words without knowledge? . . . I had
heard of thee by the hearing of the ear, but now my eye sees thee"; and
Sir 43:32–33, "The *hidden* things *are* greater (even) than these; I have
seen (but) few of His works. Everything [hath Yahweh made], And to
[the pious hath He given wisdom]."[72] Thus Humbert concludes that "Job
and Sirach go back perhaps to an Egyptian school tradition of which
Papyrus Insinger has preserved for us only a late link." Finally he
observes that, in all three—Job, Ben Sira, and *Phibis*—these "grand com-
positions" on divine providence that intend to reveal the mysteries of
God fall near the end of the respective works.

   Humbert noted the general similarities among Job, Ben Sira, and
Phibis in these "mystery demonstration" texts but he saw no detailed
similarities between Ben Sira and *Phibis*. Indeed, one must be struck with
how, if Ben Sira was using the Demotic work, some themes are not picked
up. Thus Ben Sira does not here refer to retribution and to the fool's getting
his due, nor does he mention the characteristically Egyptian heart and
tongue. There are, nevertheless, some similarities of detail that might be
noted. Thus *PIns*. xxxii2 refers to day, month, and year, and Sir 43:6
mentions months and seasons; further, God's granting welcome fresh water
is mentioned in *PIns*. xxxii6 and in Sir 43:22. Finally, both employ
mistaken statements or questions as "jumping off points" for discussions of
God's powers and beneficence. Thus the one who says, "It is not" (referring
to God's providential acts) in *PIns*. xxxi9 is referred in the lines following
to the facts of nature; similarly also Ben Sira, where the question, "Where-
fore is this?" and the mistaken statement, "This is worse than that" (Sir
39:21), also lead immediately to similar statements of God's provisioning in

---

[71] Humbert, *Sources égyptiennes*, 140.
[72] Ibid., 141–42.

nature (vv 25-27).[73] While rain and dew make their appearance in the "mystery demonstration" texts in Job (28:26; 38:28), they occur there in somewhat different contexts, and the Job texts do not mention months and seasons and do not introduce discussions of divine beneficence in nature with mistaken questions or statements. One might thus see a possibility of some limited influence of *Phibis* or of a similar text on Ben Sira here, although such influence is doubtless minor when compared to other influences: Job and a probable Egypto-Israelite tradition of such "mystery demonstration" texts used as conclusions to wisdom works.[74]

Humbert concludes his discussion of Ben Sira by noting that Ben Sira gives evidence of less influence from Egyptian wisdom than do the other Israelite wisdom works, and that only in the case of the "satire of occupations" can one see a clear case of "patent imprint." Yet he also refers to the very frequent (*"assez souvent"*) contact with *Phibis*, but regarding this contact he can conclude only that it "shows without doubt that contact between Hebraic wisdom and Egyptian wisdom had remained close until the lower epoch."[75] Could Humbert have been aware of the more recent scholarly opinion dating *Papyrus Insinger* in or before the Ptolemaic period, he might very well have evaluated the several contacts between *Phibis* and Ben Sira differently. His statement about the relationship between the two works, in fact, must appear as the strongest possible statement in view of his assumption about the date of *Papyrus Insinger*. When the work of which *Papyrus Insinger* is the primary exemplar is understood to be contemporary with or even prior to Ben Sira, then Humbert's evidence leads obviously and directly to the conclusion that Ben Sira shows more *influence* from *Phibis* than from any other Egyptian work.

Phibis *in Werner Fuss's Analysis*

After Humbert's work, the issue of the relation between Ben Sira and *Papyrus Insinger* was not taken up again until it became a topic of some significance in the 1962 Tübingen dissertation (still unpublished) of Werner Fuss, "Tradition und Komposition im Buche Jesus Sirach."[76]

---

[73] It is no accident that this similarity of style appears precisely in these mystery demonstration texts, since, as Crenshaw has shown ("The Problem of Theodicy in Sirach: On Human Bondage," *JBL* 94 [1975] 48–51), the refutation of incorrect statements is a standard element of style in Egyptian theodicies and is also employed by Ben Sira in the same way. Cf. also Crenshaw, *Wisdom*, 170–72.

[74] Crenshaw, ibid., 166–68, emphasizes that "the book of Job paved the way for 'hymnic' praise."

[75] Humbert, *Sources égyptiennes*, 143–44.

[76] In general, the dissertation attempted, without adequate criteria, to distinguish between traditional and original material in Ben Sira; cf. ibid., 28. Fuss noted (ibid., I) that Hellmut Brunner provided him assistance with Egyptian texts.

While Fuss followed Humbert in noting some (though not all) of the parallels between Ben Sira and *Phibis* to which Humbert had called attention, he also thought that he recognized several more, to an examination of which we now turn.[77]

Fuss first suggests a similarity between Sir 3:12b, "*Forsake* him (thy father) not all the days of *thy* life," and *PIns.* ii7, "Do not be bad to him in his lifetime, otherwise you will die."[78] Not only is the parallel apt, but Fuss might have noted that, just as Ben Sira and *Phibis* both include sections on the praise of the god of nature near the ends of their respective works, so both also include sections on filial piety near the first (Sir 3:1–16 and the 6th Instruction of *Phibis*, in the middle of which the extant portion of *Papyrus Insinger* begins)! Within these sections, furthermore, there are several comparable details. Thus Ben Sira, in 3:2 (and elsewhere), refers to both father and mother, as does also *PIns.* i22: "[The God-fearer is good to his fa]ther and to his mother"; and Sir 3:4 advises, "As one that layeth up treasure is he that honoureth his mother," which is very close to *PIns.* i19: "[Whoever is good to his parents, to him God gives] wealth in his purse." Further, that filial piety is God's will is emphasized in *PIns.* i22 (above) as well as in Sir 3:6b–7: "*He that obeyeth the Lord giveth rest to his mother*, And serveth his parents as masters." Sir 3:8 and *PIns.* i20, also, both connect filial piety with attendant blessings: "Honour thy father, That every blessing may overtake thee"; "[whoever is good to his parents, him] God [rewards] with blessing." Again, the idea expressed in Sir 3:10, "Glorify not thyself in the dishonour of thy father," is also expressed by *Phibis* in somewhat more detail in *PIns.* ii5, "Do not be better clothed than he (one's father) on the street, so that a stranger regards you [more than him]." Finally, both Sir 3:16b and *PIns.* ii15 refer (in different ways) to the one who curses his mother.

There can be no doubt whatsoever that Ben Sira has thought here of the fifth commandment,[79] and one may also note certain similarities between some of his statements here and similar statements in the Book of Proverbs. Thus Sir 3:2, "The Lord hath given the father glory as touching the children, And hath established the judgement of the mother as touching the sons,"· recalls similar statements in Proverbs where it is underscored that the counsel of father and mother is to be kept. Thus Prov 1:8 admonishes, "Hear, my son, your father's instruction (*mwsr*), and reject not your mother's teaching"; similarly Prov 6:20. Further, just as Sir 3:16b condemns cursing one's mother, so also does Prov 20:20 (where it is *father* and mother). Beyond these similarities between Ben

---

[77] I omit here mention of those parallels noted by Fuss to which Humbert also called attention.

[78] Fuss, "Tradition und Komposition," 49.

[79] So also Middendorp, *Stellung*, 59.

Sira and his Judaic tradition, however—indeed, precisely because of them—the other similarities between Ben Sira and *Phibis*, not the least of which is the placing within their respective works of these sections on filial piety, stand out.[80]

In 2:1–6 Ben Sira explains that a testing is the necessary prelude to the acquisition of wisdom, and Fuss considers this similar to *PIns.* xii14:22;[81] yet this section of *Phibis* speaks rather of one's testing of different persons in different types of relationships. The two sections hardly deal with the same theme.

I can see no connection between Sir 4:29–31 and *PIns.* xxi3–4.[82]

There is a stylistic connection between Sir 5:14a, "Be not called 'Double-tongued,'" and a list of admonitions in *PIns.* iii2–8, all of which lines begin, "Be careful that you are not called . . ."[83] Thus, e.g., line 6, "Be careful that you are not called 'gossip.'"

Fuss also finds a parallel to *PIns.* xii14–22 in Sir 6:7, "If thou *acquirest* a friend *acquire him by testing*,"[84] and here he is on better ground than when proposing (above) that the same section of *Phibis* found a parallel in Sir 2:1–6. Each line in this section of *Phibis* begins, "One does not get to know . . . ," and then indicates the type of person one might wish to know, followed by the kind of testing that is required for such knowledge. Thus *PIns.* xii15, "One does not get to know the heart of a smart man if one has not tested him somehow"; or line 18, "One does not get to know the heart of a companion if one has not asked him for advice in need." One will have to agree that especially *PIns.* xii18 is as close to Sir 6:7a as is Xenophon,[85] and that statements of this sentiment are not found in the Book of Proverbs or in Theognis.[86] Fuss's observation thus supports the conjecture made on pp. 70–71, above.

Fuss is correct in citing as a parallel to Sir 7:23a, "Hast thou sons, correct them," *PIns.* ix9, "A son does not die from blows at the hand of the father"; nevertheless, Prov 13:24 is closer.[87]

Fuss connects Sir 7:32, "To the poor stretch out thy hand, That thy blessing may be perfected," with *PIns.* xvi13, "Whoever gives food to the poor, him God receives to himself in eternal grace."[88] We have

---

[80] Middendorp, ibid., 80, finds a similarity between Prov 17:16b and Sir 3:11a. While a relationship is possible, it is less certain, since the maxims are formulated differently, and Ben Sira speaks of *kbwd*, whereas Proverbs refers to the sons' *tp'rt*.

[81] Fuss, "Tradition und Komposition," 56.

[82] Ibid., 59.

[83] Ibid., 62.

[84] Ibid., 64. Cf. above, pp. 64–65.

[85] Above, p. 44.

[86] Cf. above, pp. 4 and 30–31.

[87] Fuss, "Tradition und Komposition," 71; cf. above, pp. 6, 72.

[88] Fuss, "Tradition und Komposition," 73.

already, however, had occasion to note Prov 22:9 in this connection.[89]

The next parallel noted by Fuss between Ben Sira and *Phibis* is *PIns.* iv2, "Haste not to seek battle against the strong and mighty lord," and Sir 8:1–3:

> Contend not with a mighty man,
> > *Lest thou return to his hand.*
> *Contend not with one that is sterner than thou,*
> > Lest thou fall into his hand.
> *Devise not against a* man that is rich.[90]
> > Lest he weigh thy price, and thou be destroyed.
> For gold hath made many reckless,
> > And wealth hath led astray the hearts of princes.
> Quarrel not with a loud-mouthed man,
> > And put not wood on fire.[91]

While the Book of Proverbs provides a certain parallel to Ben Sira at this point (Prov 26:20–21: "For lack of wood the fire goes out; and where there is no whisperer, quarreling ceases. As charcoal to hot embers and wood to fire, so is a quarrelsome man for kindling strife."), it is nevertheless true that Ben Sira and *Phibis* are extremely close both in the aspect of caution which they propose[92] and also in the specifics of their advice. Thus one should also note the following line of *Phibis, PIns.* iv3, "Whoever throws his [breas]t against the lance, into him the thrust goes."[93]

Fuss has misunderstood Sir 8:5–7, but his association of *PIns.* iii15, "Do not associate much with the evil person, because he has made a name for himself (or is eminent)," with those verses is at least partially appropriate for Sir 8:4: "Associate not with a foolish man, Lest he despise *princes.*"[94]

Fuss is, of course, correct in seeing a parallel between Sir 8:15–16,

> *Walk* not with a cruel man,
> > Lest thou be overwhelmed with misfortune:
> For he will *walk with his face to the front,*

---

[89] Cf. above, pp. 65–66.

[90] The Hebrew reads, "a man that is not rich"—clearly an error in view of the following statements.

[91] Fuss, "Tradition und Komposition," 73–74.

[92] Cf. above, pp. 17–19.

[93] One may also mention Qoh 8:2–5 as a more distant parallel.

[94] Fuss, "Tradition und Komposition," 74–75. There seems to be something wrong with the second stich of the Hebrew line, for which none of the suggested emendations appears quite satisfactory. (Duesberg et Auvray, *Ecclésiastique*, also Spicq, "Ecclésiastique," seem merely to follow the Latin; Peters, *Jesus Sirach*, follows the Hebrew with hesitation.) I have considered whether Ben Sira might have mistranslated *Phibis* at this point, but the word *rn* (name) is so common that a mistranslation is hardly likely, and, in *Insinger* in any case, it is very well written. One might also raise the possibility of a damaged MS, but the most likely explanation is the most common, that the Hebrew MS tradition is corrupt at this point.

> And through his foolishness thou wilt *be destroyed.*
> *If he is a man of anger do not bring your brow into safety,*
>   And ride not with him *on the road.*
> For blood is as nothing in his eyes,
>   And where there is no helper, he will destroy thee,

and *PIns.* xii6 and xxvi12: "Do not trust a stranger on the way, if no people are near you. . . . Do not deal with another in whose heart hate is."[95] There is a good chance, however, that Ben Sira is here simply rephrasing Prov 4:14, 16:

> Do not enter the path of the wicked,
>   and do not walk in the way of evil men.
>
> . . . .
>
> For they cannot sleep unless they have done wrong;
>   they are robbed of sleep unless they have made some one
>   stumble.

Fuss is also correct in connecting *PIns.* iii14, "Do not join with the one who is [great]er than you, else your life will perish," with Sir 9:13a, b: "Keep far from the man that hath power to kill, and *thou wilt not be in* terror of death's terrors."[96] While Prov 16:14 and 20:2 both warn of the king's wrath (*'ymh, hmh*), they lack the specific note of caution expressed by both Ben Sira and *Phibis* in their "stay away from." Thus we again find Ben Sira and *Phibis* agreeing both in their note of caution and in the specifics of that caution. Both *Phibis* and Ben Sira, further-more, refer generally to the one who is "greater" or has "power," not to the more specific "king" of Proverbs.

Fuss also sees a parallel between Sir 11:25, "A day's *goodness* mak-eth *evil* to be forgotten, And a day's *evil* maketh *goodness* to be forgot-ten; *And the last end of a person will be upon him,*" and *PIns.* xx1, "The time of perishing perishes if the person's name remains pre-served."[97] While there is considerable similarity of sentiment between those two proverbs (in 11:22–28 Ben Sira writes of death as the final judging point regarding the quality of one's life), *Phibis's* characteristi-cally Egyptian reference to the reward of name immortality is not to be found here in Ben Sira. Precisely this note *is* struck in Ben Sira, however, in his climactic statement in 41:12–13:

> Be in fear for thy name, for that abideth longer for thee
>   Than thousands of treasure of *wisdom.*
> *The value of a* life lasts for *a number of* days,
>   But the *value* of a name for days without number.

95 Fuss, "Tradition und Komposition," 76.
96 Ibid., 80.
97 Ibid., 91.

Phibis thus expresses, in *PIns.* xx1, one of Ben Sira's central sage themes—the enduring importance of the name![98]

In 11:29–34 Ben Sira offers advice on staying away from various kinds of potentially harmful persons, with which section Fuss compares *PIns.* xxix16, "There is found also no medicine for the tongue of an evil person."[99] This is certainly a part of Ben Sira's sentiment; one may note especially 11:29b, "How many are the wounds of a slanderer," and v 31, "The backbiter turneth good into evil, And in thy *desirable* qualities he putteth a *conspiracy.*"

"Do not trust your enemy," in *PIns.* xii8, Fuss finds parallel to Sir 12:10, "Never trust an enemy."[100] One would be inclined to reject any significance for this parallel altogether (nearly everyone learns it by age 12) were it not for the fact that the line in *Phibis* occurs within a section which has several lines of connection with Sir 6:5–17 (cf. again the discussion above, pp. 64–65). Intriguing here is also the fact that the Greek and Syriac of Ben Sira both also read, "*your* enemy."[101] Does *Phibis* then provide (as source of the proverb) a third attestation for that reading in Ben Sira? The sentiment is so thoroughly universal, however, that any judgment about dependence must remain suspended.

Another parallel to Ben Sira may be found in *PIns.* x12–13:[102] "Do not draw near, if it is not time for it, else your Lord will hate you; (but also) do not be far removed, lest one must seek you and you cause stink in the heart of your lord," which Fuss correctly connects to Sir 13:9–10:

> Doth a noble draw near? keep at a distance—
> And so much the more will he cause thee to approach.
> Do not thyself draw near, lest thou be put at a distance;
> And keep not (too) far away, lest *thou be hated.*

It appears likely that Ben Sira has here conflated Prov 25:6–7 with *PIns.* x12–13,[103] since Sir 13:9b, 10a coincides fairly closely with Prov 25:7 ("It is better to be told, 'Come up here,' than to be put lower"), whereas v 10 (Do not draw near; do not be too far away) repeats the themes of *PIns.* x12–13.[104]

I can find no connection between Sir 15:6b and *PIns.* ii2.[105]

The next parallel noted by Fuss is between Sir 18:33, "Be not a

---

[98] Cf. the discussion above, pp. 17–19.
[99] Fuss, "Tradition und Komposition," 92.
[100] Ibid., 95.
[101] So also Duesberg et Auvray, *Ecclésiastique*, Spicq, "Ecclésiastique."
[102] Fuss, "Tradition und Komposition," 99. Cf. also my earlier note, "A Hellenistic Egyptian Parallel to Ben Sira," *JBL* 97 (1978) 257–58.
[103] Cf. above, p. 8.
[104] Cf. on this parallel further below, pp. 92–93
[105] Fuss, "Tradition und Komposition," 106.

squanderer and a drunkard, Else there will be nothing in *[thy]* purse," and *PIns.* iv6–7: "Do not be a spendthrift if you possess little and do not have a reserve behind you. Do not squander the excess of an undertaking before fate has given it to you."[106] The admonitions are certainly close.

Fuss finds similarities between Sir 6:7–12, 13–18, a section on bad women and on the good/beautiful woman, and *PIns.* viii19.[107] In reality, a considerable section of *Phibis, PIns.* viii4–19, is relevant to Ben Sira here:

> 4 If a woman is beautiful, your lord is revealed in her.
> 5 A good woman, who does not love another in the neighborhood, is of value as the wife of a wise man. A woman with good character is a treasury.
> 6 Women who are bad in the above relationship do not become prosperous,
> 7 for what is good in the house happens through the woman.
> 8 There are women who fill their house with wealth without buying anything.
> 9 There are women who, as lady of the house—because of their character—become ladies of praise.
> 10 There are those who are described in the book, "Faults of Women."
> 11 Fear them very much out of fear for the Lady of [Love], Hathor.
>
> . . . .
>
> 13 Whoever is worthy before the heart of God receives a proper (wife).
>
> . . . .
>
> 15 The woman who is praised by a stranger is not a good woman.
> 16 (Nevertheless), the woman who behaves incorrectly on the street need not be a street whore.
> 17 (Yet) whoever has a rendezvous with such a one is not a smart man.
>
> . . . .
>
> 19 There are among women upon earth good and bad; the proper and the bad woman are determined by the command of [God].

While Ben Sira is more organized, presenting in 26:6–12 his own catalog of "faults of women" and in vv 13–18 praise of a good or beautiful woman, there are several points of contact. Ben Sira writes,

> 6 Grief of heart and sorrow is the wife jealous of (another) wife,
>   A scourge of the tongue *communicating to all.*
> 7 Like a hard joke is a wicked woman:
>   He that taketh hold of her is as one that graspeth a scorpion.

---

[106] Ibid., 124.
[107] Ibid., 163–64.

8 Great wrath (doth) a drunken woman (cause);
   She doth not cover her own shame.
9 The whoredom of a woman is in the lifting up of her eyes,
   And she will be known by her eyelids.
10 Upon a headstrong daughter keep strict watch,
   Lest, finding liberty, she use it for herself.
11 Look well after a shameless eye,
   And marvel not if it trespass against thee.
12 As a thirsty traveller that openeth his mouth,
   And drinketh of any water that is near,
   So she sitteth down at every post,
   And openeth [her] quiver to an arrow.
13 The grace of a wife *benefitteth* her husband,
   And her understanding fatteneth his bones.[108]
15 Grace upon grace is a shamefast woman,
   And *lips that are mum are priceless.*[109]
16 The sun arising in the highest places,
   Is *a beautiful woman in the chamber of her young man.*
17 A lamp *burning* on the holy candlestick,
   Is the *splendor* of a face on a *measured height.*[110]
18 Golden pillars upon *a* silver base,
   Are beautiful feet upon *well turned* heels.

Thus, while there are obvious differences between Ben Sira and *Phibis* in their characterizations of women (Ben Sira is interested only in the women of the household: wife and daughter; *Phibis* speaks of women in general), both refer to the benefit to the home of the good wife, and both emphasize sexual promiscuity as a main aspect of the bad woman. In the Book of Proverbs, of course, one finds the praise of the good wife in Prov 31:10–31, where the benefits of the good wife are described at length, and 11:22: "A gold ring in a swine's snout is a beautiful woman without discretion,"[111] which one might compare with Sir 26:6; and Qoh 7:26, 28 expresses a general misogyny; but the contrasting portrait belongs to *Phibis* and Ben Sira.

There could well be some connection between *PIns.* xxviii1, "Little work and little nourishment are better than fulness while you are abroad," and Sir 29:22: "Better the life of the poor under a shelter of logs, Than sumptuous fare *among* strangers."[112] (Prov 12:9, "Better is a man of humble standing who works for himself than one who plays the great man but lacks bread," is a maxim in a similar vein but lacks the "better poor at home than rich abroad" theme of Ben Sira and *Phibis*.)

---

108 Verse 14 does not occur in the Hebrew text, and I omit it here.
109 Literally: "No price for a tied up mouth."
110 The reference is apparently to a neck like a stately pillar. See the next line.
111 Cf. Volz, *Hiob und Weisheit*, 192.
112 Fuss, "Tradition und Komposition," 179.

We saw above that Sir 30:1-13 and *PIns*. viii21-ix20 expressed somewhat similar ideas about the rearing of a son, but that Ben Sira probably relied primarily on Judaic proverbial tradition.[113] Fuss, however, emphasizes the similarity between Sir 30:7, "He that pampereth his son shall bind up his wounds, And his *bowels* tremble at every cry," and *PIns*. ix10: "Whoever protects his son with love so much that he perishes, perishes with him."[114] These aphorisms are certainly close, and one will thus surely have to reckon with the possibility that Ben Sira has, in 30:1-13, blended Judaic tradition with the advice of *Phibis*.

Regarding Sir 30:21, Fuss cites,[115] in addition to the lines from *Phibis* cited by Humbert,[116] *PIns*. xx7, but this line also speaks of the theme of sorrow and is thus irrelevant.[117]

Sir 37:14 and *PIns*. iv23 and xxv18 all refer to the heart and its central role in human existence,[118] but only Ben Sira here refers to the heart's actively giving advice.

Sir 40:11a, "All things that are from the earth return to the earth," is exactly the same as *PIns*. xxx6, "What comes forth from the earth also returns to it."[119] In both cases this could be no more than a widely repeated Hellenistic saying; thus Middendorp cites, along with several less appropriate Hellenic sayings, Aesch. *Cho*. 127 (he means 127-28),[120] "Earth too, herself, who bringeth all things to birth and fosters them to take them back . . .";[121] but in reality Sir 40:11 probably relies on Qoh 12:7: "The dust returns to the earth as it was, and the spirit returns to God who gave it." Both express the theme of "earth to earth and spirit to air," since Sir 40:11b continues: "And what is from on high (returneth) on high."[122]

Fuss also calls attention, in addition to the parallels noted above, to four stylistic similarities between Ben Sira and *Phibis*. The first is the presence in both texts, and in *Amenemope*, of thematic units ("*Sinneinheiten*") of advice.[123] Thus Ben Sira's tendency to organize his practical advice into groups of proverbs is paralleled by the chapter divisions of *Phibis* and of *Amenemope*.[124] Also, one may note that both texts use

---

[113] Above, pp. 69-72.
[114] Fuss, "Tradition und Komposition," 181.
[115] Ibid., 184-85.
[116] Cf. above, pp. 72-73.
[117] Cf. above, p. 73.
[118] Fuss, "Tradition und Komposition," 216-17.
[119] Ibid., 236.
[120] Middendorp, *Stellung*, 23.
[121] Text and ET in *The Choephoroi of Aeschylus* (Cambridge: University Press, 1901).
[122] Cf. also *Ps.-Phoc.* 107-8.
[123] Fuss, "Tradition und Komposition," 275.
[124] Cf. the discussion of this characteristic of Ben Sira's and its relation to the Judaic wisdom tradition above, pp. 14-16, 24, 54.

series of warnings and exhortations,[125] e.g., Sir 4:23–28:

> Withhold not *(thy) word forever,*
> > And hide not thy wisdom.
> For Wisdom is known through utterance,
> > And understanding by the *answer* of the tongue.
> *Do not rebel against God,*
> > And be humble toward God.
> Be not ashamed to *turn from iniquity,*
> > And stand not against the stream.
> *Incline* not thy soul *to* a fool.
> > And *do not refuse before rulers.*
> *Do not sit with an unjust judge,*
> > For you *will judge according to his good pleasure.*
> Strive for *righteousness* until death,
> > And the Lord will fight for thee.
> *Be not called "Double-tongued,"*
> > *And do not slander your tongue;*

or 7:1–26, or, in *Phibis, PIns.* col. iii:

> Be careful that you are not called "the evil man" because of evil
> mercilessness; do not be voracious.
> Be careful that you are not called "the impudent one" because of a
> shameful appearance of which you, yourself, are not aware.
> Be careful that you are not called "fool" because of voraciousness
> because you do not keep a tight rein on yourself.
> Be careful that you are not called "the one who collects by debt-
> arrest" because of brutality.
> Be careful that you are not called "gossip" because your tongue is in
> every house.
>
> . . . .
>
> Do not do what excites you with a woman in order to deceive her; do
> not flatter another man's boy lover.
> Do not speak your mind [literally: heart] noisily in a conversation in a
> large crowd.
> Do not speak with loud voice if a superior hears your voice (or is
> nearby).
>
> (*PIns.* iii2–6, 9–11)

While this phenomenon occurs in the Book of Proverbs, it is limited
to 24:13–22; even chaps. 1–9 mingle such exhortations and warnings
with maxims, as does Qoh 5:1–9. One does find a brief list of such exhortations in Qoh 9:7–9. Such lists of warnings or exhortations do not occur
in Theognis. Is this simply a Ptolemaic period Egypto-Judaic trait, or has
Ben Sira been influenced directly by *Phibis?*

---

[125] Fuss, "Tradition und Komposition," 278.

Fuss next refers to the collections of *yš* sayings in Ben Sira 19 and 20 and in *PIns.* v20–23.[126] Thus Sir 20:9–12:

> *There* is advantage for a man to be in adversity,
>> And *there is discovery unto loss.*
> There is a gift that profiteth thee nothing,
>> And *there is* a gift *of which the return is* double.
> *There is* loss *on account of* honour,
>> And *there is one that hath lifted up [his] head from*
>> *humiliation.*
> *There is one that buyeth* much for little
>> And *one who* pays *for it* sevenfold;

and *PIns.* v20–23:

> There are people who cannot eat and (still) in their heart want much
>> food.
> There is, however, the one who is sick from the preceding day and
>> (still) desires wine.
> [There are] also people who allege hating fornication and (still)
>> distribute among women what they have over.
> Some die in misery because of voraciousness.

Again, the form of the *yš* saying occurs several times in the Book of Proverbs, as well as with some frequency in Ben Sira, but it is this stylistic trait of running several such sayings together around one theme which Ben Sira and *Phibis* have in common.

Finally, Fuss notes that Ben Sira, somewhat similarly to *Phibis's* pattern of placing a summary line just before his standard chapter closing line, often closes a thematic section "with a religious expression" or with other "concluding thoughts."[127] *Phibis's* pattern is to close each chapter with the statement, "The fortune and fate that come are determined by God" (*PIns.* v11; conclusion of the 7th Instruction), or with a minor variation of that statement, and to place just before this standard conclusion a summary statement related to the chapter, e.g., *PCarlsberg* IIii16–17 (substituted for *PIns.* v10), "The fool who does not speak, his voice is not heard, since he is silent and he is not questioned," in keeping with the theme of constancy (*PIns.* ii22) of the 7th Instruction; or *PIns.* vii17–18, "God gives wealth in reserve without (your) receiving; he creates, on the other hand, poverty in a purse without (your) excessive expense," concluding the 8th Instruction, on "not being voracious, lest you become a companion of poverty" (*PIns.* v12). Ben Sira's use of closing summary statements was discussed above in chap. 1,[128] and we

---

126 Ibid., 278.
127 Ibid., 278–79.
128 Above, pp. 15–16.

may simply refer here again to Sir 7:36; 28:6; 35:10; and 37:15.

Having called attention to so many parallels between Ben Sira and *Phibis*, Fuss was careful not to overstate his case. Thus he referred to "patent . . . connections but not direct dependencies," but he was willing to state of the "connections": "That they are an expression of Palestinian-Egyptian cultural relationships in the period of the Ptolemies appears . . . clear to me."[129] It seems to me, however, that Fuss may have been overly cautious, and that he probably left the statement of "connections" or "relationships" too general. His explanation of the relationships between Ben Sira and *Phibis* is essentially the same as that of Humbert; but Humbert was under the impression that *Phibis* was written two centuries later than Ben Sira, whereas Fuss accepted Volten's dating of *Papyrus Insinger* in the Ptolemaic period or earlier.[130] This earlier dating of the Demotic work and the recognition of further close parallels between it and Ben Sira, in addition to those noted by Humbert, should have led to a rethinking of the nature of the "connections," but this has not been the case.[131] Before, however, any more definite conclusions can be proposed, other parallels between the two works need to be described.

Further Evidence of Borrowing

B. Couroyer has proposed that Sir 4:11, "Wisdom instructeth her sons, And *teacheth* all who give heed to her," contains an "Egyptianism," since the pair of terms *lmd* piel (instruct) and *'wd* hiphil (teach, literally: admonish) correspond to the frequent Egyptian pair *sbȝ* and *mtr*.[132] Among the Egyptian texts in which these terms occur together, Couroyer cites *PIns.*

---

[129] Fuss, "Tradition und Komposition," 279.

[130] Ibid.

[131] Cf. also Marböck, *Weisheit im Wandel,* 169–70.

[132] B. Couroyer, "Un égyptianisme dans Ben Sira IV, 11," *RB* 82 (1975) 206–17. Lévi, *Ecclésiastique* 2, and Segal, *Spr Bn Syr'* (cf. the references in Gordis, *The Song of Songs and Lamentations. A Study, Modern Translation and Commentary* [New York: KTAV, 1974] 164) take *t'yd* to refer to strengthening, as does also Gordis, ibid., in his discussion of Lam 2:13. The sense of "strengthen," to be sure, would fit Ben Sira's line, but the assumption of synonymous parallelism in v 11 is rendered more likely by v 12: "They that love her . . . they that seek her"; thus "instructeth" and "*teacheth*," not "instructeth" and "strengtheneth," are made more likely for v 11. The Greek reads *epilambanetai* and the Syriac *tnhr,* leading Box and Oesterley, *APOT* 1, and Gordis, *Song of Songs and Lamentations,* 164, to assume that the Greek has correctly translated the Hebrew. Box and Oesterley then follow the Syriac for their translation—"enlighteneth"—and assume a corresponding Hebrew original of *t'yr* instead of *t'yd* (after Smend, *Weisheit*). D. Barthélemy and O. Rickenbacher, however, in their *Konkordanz zum hebräischen Sirach* (Göttingen: Vandenhoeck & Ruprecht, 1973) 289, relate *t'yd* to *h'yd* in 46:19, where the Greek translates *epemartyrato*; and this is the sense one would expect from BDB, where the hiphil of *'ûd* (vb. denom. from *'dh,* "testimony, witness") can mean "exhort solemnly, admonish, charge, . . . enjoin solemnly." This corresponds exactly to the Egyptian *mtr,* which normally means "testify, bear witness," but also, as here in *Phibis,* "teach."

viii21–22: "The 10th Instruction: The instruction not to become tired in teaching your son. A stone statue is the dumb son whom his father has not taught."[133] Perhaps we have here yet another case of Ben Sira's reliance on *Phibis*, since these lines of *Phibis* not only contain the comparable terms, but also refer to the teaching of sons.

Fuss called attention to the parallel between Sir 13:9–10 and *PIns*. x12–13,[134] but there is actually a series of running parallels in these respective sections, and it will be instructive to examine the relevant lines here side by side, along with Prov. 25:6–7.

Sir 13:9–13		Prov 25:6–7
9 Doth a noble draw near? keep at a distance—		Do not *claim honor* in the king's presence or stand in the place of the great;
And so much the more will he cause thee to approach.		for it is better to be told, "Come up here," than to be
10 Do not thyself draw near lest thou be put at a distance;	*PIns.* x12–xi23 12 Do not draw near, if it is not time for it, else your lord will hate you;	put lower in the presence of the prince.
And keep not (too) far away, lest *thou be hated.* [Note "hate" in *PIns.* x12.]	13 (but also) do not be far removed, lest one must seek you and you cause stink in the heart of your lord.	
11 Venture not to be free with him,	20 Say not a word at all to him if anger is in his heart.	
And mistrust his much conversation	23 Hasten not to do something wicked if he says something which it is not proper to obey.	
For *in his much* conversation *there are tests.*	xi1 Do not be forgetful at the time of questioning.	
And when he smileth at thee he is probing thee.	3 Do not answer if he asks you about something with which you are not acquainted.	

[133] Couroyer, "Egyptianisme," 211 n. 18.

[134] Cf. above, p. 85. The theme of proper, indeed cautious behavior before rulers is of course related to the upper-class orientation of wisdom literature (made clear by Gordis, "Social Background"), and related examples can be found in both Israel and Egypt. Cf., e.g., Qoh 8:2–5 and *Ptahhotep* 120. The exact correspondences, however, between *Phibis* and Ben Sira go beyond this general thematic similarity.

8   Do not be ashamed if,
    at the time of an
    accusation, he
    questions and
    interrogates you.

13 Take heed and be   23   Do not trust the one
    wary,   whom you do not
                                       know in your heart,
    And go not about   lest he deceitfully
    with men of   cheat you.
    violence.

While both Ben Sira and *Phibis* make other statements within these sections which are not found here in both, what is remarkable about these sections is that so many similar statements are made in both *in the same order*! This is an almost certain sign of borrowing.

We noted in chap. 1 that one of the most prominent and relatively unique aspects of Ben Sira's work is his shame-based caution and an attendant interest in preserving and guarding one's good name.[135] The prominence of exactly this same complex of themes in *Phibis* can also be detailed. In the preceding discussion it has already been noted that a statement of particular caution in Sir 5:14 is paralleled stylistically in *PIns.* iii2–8 and in content in iii6,[136] and that the theme of testing a friend is similar in both.[137] We have also seen that the two works agree that one should "contend not with a mighty man,"[138] and that both agree that one should, in fact, approach persons in power or authority with caution.[139] The importance of the name was noted in *PIns.* xx1,[140] and also the importance of staying away from various kinds of potentially harmful persons.[141] Further, that one should stay not too close and not too far away from one's lord is emphasized in both texts.[142] One may note, also, *PIns.* xiii9: "Do not join yourself to a thief, lest you fall into misfortune." The 15th Instruction of *Phibis*, further, puts caution, name, and, in a sense, shame together when it gives as a title for the instruction, "Be not avaricious, lest your name stink" (*PIns.* xv7). While all of the 15th Instruction does not, then, deal with this theme, one must note especially *PIns.* xv13, "Avarice banishes shame, mercy, and trust from the heart."

Quite to the point are two lines in *PIns.* ix1–2: "A youth [who] does not perish because of his stomach is not reproached; he who is innocent

---

135 Above, pp. 17–19.
136 Above, p. 82.
137 Above, p. 82.
138 Above, p. 83.
139 Above, p. 83.
140 Above, pp. 84–85.
141 Above, p. 84.
142 Above, p. 85; cf. also the immediately preceding discussion, pp. 92–93.

with regard to his phallus, his name does not stink." Here all the themes of caution, of shame, and of the importance of one's name come together in a way highly reminiscent of Ben Sira. In *PIns.* ix8, further, shame and caution are again placed together in a way similar to that of Ben Sira: "The youth who is cautious because of shame will not receive bad thrashings"; and in *PIns.* iii3, in the first section we have in *Papyrus Insinger*, the author makes shame an important ingredient of the advised caution: "Be careful that you are not called 'the impudent one' because of a shameful appearance of which you, yourself, are not aware." Very significantly *PIns.* ix7 informs us that Thoth "created shame for the smart person so that he might avoid everything bad." While Ben Sira does not speak of shame as God-given, he nevertheless connects it with the sage and with righteousness; thus *Phibis* is here very close to Ben Sira's thought.

One may read, further, in *PIns.* ix23 that "light anger, shamefastness, and reliability are the honor of a wise man"; and *PIns.* xxvii3 advises, "Better is a death in poverty than a life without shame." Perhaps the strongest statement in Phibis about the importance of shame is *PIns.* xiii4–5: "Shame is a gift of God to the man whom one can trust; he does not give it as a portion to the wicked or impious person." Finally, two other statements in Phibis emphasize the importance of one's name and the immortality of a good name. *PIns.* xvi9 says that "the good repute of the good man disseminates a good name from one to the other"; and ii12 asserts that "the resuscitation of the heart of the dead (person) leaves his name [behind] on earth." This last is exceedingly close to what Ben Sira says of the fathers in Sir 44:8: "Some of them there are who have left a name, That men might tell of *it in their inheritance.*" Naturally, Ben Sira does not take over here the Egyptian concept of life after death, which involved the "resuscitation of the heart." (One will recall that Ben Sira's views on shame were summarized in chap. 1.)[143]

While the Florentine fragments of *Phibis* offer scant additional material from the book (they duplicate, for the most part, portions of lines from *Papyrus Insinger* and from the *Carlsberg Papyri* of *Phibis*),[144] fragments 1 and 2 do contain portions of the opening of the work, otherwise unknown. Here, in fragment 2, line 5, one may read, "T]eaching about shame." Thus, in spite of the otherwise very incomplete state of the fragment, we have yet another attestation to *Phibis*'s considerable interest in shame.

A final parallel perhaps allows us to observe Ben Sira's process of selection and utilization at work. The 14th Instruction of *Phibis* is

---

[143] Cf. above, pp. 17–19.
[144] Cf. G. Botti and A. Volten, "Florentiner-Fragmente zum Texte des Pap. Insinger," *AcOr* 25 (1960) 29–42.

entitled, "Give no inferior man power lest he cause thy name to become foolish" (*PIns.* xiv3). Following, then, two lines (xiv4–5) which make general statements about this theme, we encounter six lines (xiv6–11) which are fairly closely parallel to a section of Ben Sira in which he advocates rather harsh treatment of slaves:

> 6 If the fool does not seé a rod before him there is no concern in his heart.
> 7 The fool who has no care makes care for the one who commissioned him.
> 8 The reward which the inferior man receives, let it be food and rod for him.
> 9 A foolish man who lowers his gaze is well trained.
> 10 If a foolish man has no work, his phallus leaves him no rest.
> 11 If the rod is far from the master his servant does not obey him.

With these lines may be compared Sir 33:24–28:

> Fodder and *whip* and burden for an ass,
>> *And rebelliousness means* work for a servant!
> Put thy servant to work *that he not* seek rest;
>> *And if he has raised up his head he will deal treacherously*
>> *with you.*
> Yoke and *cord are a rod keeping him.*
> Put thy servant to work, that he not *rebel*;
>> For *sluggishness effects the multiplying of evil.*
> For an evil servant *multiply his bonds.*

Both in Ben Sira and *Phibis*, then, we have harsh treatment proposed for the slave, along with the double-sided rationale for such treatment: The slave must be kept burdened in order to keep his mind on his business; idleness breeds mischief. Furthermore, the statements in both works that a slave's wages are food and rod (or whip) and that yoke, cord, and rod keep the slave in line are quite close. After this advice, however, *Phibis* goes on to explain the problems of having a slave in a position of authority or control, in keeping with the theme of the chapter, but Ben Sira makes a sudden and abrupt change in his advice about slaves. After recommending, in 33:28, multiplied bonds for the evil slave, he suddenly, in v 29, calls for equity and justice. "*Do not show preeminence over any man,*" he counsels, "And *without judgment* do nothing." Then he begins to counsel treatment of slaves that seems to be exactly the opposite of that in vv 24–28. "*Let thy one* servant," he now advises in v 30, "be as thyself," and he continues,

> Treat *thy one servant like a* brother—
>> Be not jealous *of thy life's blood.*
> *For if* thou treat him ill, *he will go forth and perish.*
>> On what way shalt thou find him?
>>> (Sir 33:31)

Not only do these lines have no parallel in *Phibis*, they express a viewpoint not to be found, if we may trust Robert Gordis on the subject, "in any other branch of Oriental Wisdom, except the Babylonian."[145] The language Ben Sira uses here, however, is reminiscent of something in the Torah.

Lev 25:39 refers to the "brother," i.e., fellow Hebrew as a hired servant, and v 46 again refers to "brother" servants and enjoins harsh treatment in their case. It is thus possible that Ben Sira brings to bear, in 33:30-31, ideas derived from the Torah, although the connection is not close enough to raise that possibility to the level of certainty. The idea of kindness to slaves was otherwise current, one may note, in Hellenistic Judaism. Thus Pseudo-Phocylides 223-26 advises,

> Provide your slave with the tribute he owes to his stomach.
> Apportion to a slave what is appointed so that he will be as you wish.
> Insult not your slave by branding him.
> Do not hurt a slave by slandering him to his master.[146]

Aside from the general concept of kindness, however, there are no lines of connection between these verses and Sir 33:30-31, and the slave as brother is not mentioned, so that Leviticus 25 remains a likely source for Ben Sira's thought here.[147] Finally, of course, Ben Sira closes with his characteristic self-interest motivation: Treat your servant badly enough, and he will run away, and then you'll be without.

In this section, then, Ben Sira brings three elements together: advice to treat slaves harshly, advice to treat slaves gently, and self-interest motivation in support of the second advice. The first closely parallels a section of *Phibis* and may be derived from there. The second has another origin, possibly the Torah. The last is very characteristic of Ben Sira's basic philosophy. We probably see here, therefore—just as we saw in the case of the use of Theognis—how Ben Sira appropriates foreign material and juxtaposes it to traditional Judaic themes or to his characteristic eudaemonism or caution, or, as in this case, to both.[148]

At his point it will be instructive simply to do some counting. In the discussion of Theognis parallels to Ben Sira, a total of fifty-two lines in Theognis—or, if one counts the entire section on drinking, Theog. 467-510, eighty-seven lines—were found to be quite closely parallel to

---

[145] Gordis, "Social Background," 115.

[146] The translation is that of P. W. van der Horst, *The Sentences of Pseudo-Phocylides*, 255-57.

[147] Job, in his defense (31:13-15), affirms that he has always dealt justly with slaves, and that one God made both master and slave. While this does reveal a positive side in the Judaic wisdom tradition regarding treatment of slaves, it is hardly Ben Sira's slave as brother.

[148] Box and Oesterley, *APOT* 1, see the shift as a change in topic from a discussion of many slaves to one of only one slave.

lines in Ben Sira.[149] Of the fifty-two, twenty-four dealt with the one theme of caution in friendship and eleven (all but two from one section) with the theme of caution in drinking. On the basis of the closeness between these lines and certain portions of Ben Sira we were able to conclude that Ben Sira had relied on Theognis for certain maxims and admonitions. We also found that, while Ben Sira apparently used certain maxims from Theognis with which he agreed and for which he apparently had no other source, nothing in Theognis seems to have changed or influenced his basic theological position.[150] In *Phibis*, however, we have been able to note sixty-eight lines containing maxims and advice fairly close to statements in Ben Sira and, further, an additional fifty-eight lines in *sections* connected in some relevant way to Ben Sira.[151] (This is without counting the long creation hymn in *PIns.* xxx18–xxxiii6, which is related to Ben Sira in regard to order.) *Papyrus Insinger*, however, contains only 814 lines, whereas Theognis, Book 1, contains 1230; thus the fifty-two lines of Theognis referred to above as quite close to Ben Sira represent just over four per cent of Theognis (precisely, 4.23%), whereas the 126 lines of *Phibis* represent over fifteen per cent (precisely, 15.48%) of *Papyrus Insinger*! Furthermore, four sections of *Phibis* (on filial piety, on the poverty produced by desire, on good and bad women, and on the treatment of slaves), as opposed to one section of Theognis, find counterparts in Ben Sira. When one adds to these observations the similarities in order—both the overall order (filial piety near the first, creation hymn near the end) and the individual similarity of order (the sections on caution in dealing with rulers)—and finally the four stylistic similarities to which Fuss pointed (even granting that these appear in at least incipient stages in the Judaic wisdom tradition prior to Ben Sira), one has a very weighty case for direct relationship. On top of all this, one finds in *Phibis* exactly Ben Sira's characteristic ethics of caution based on shame and regard for one's name, *a similarity which cannot be paralleled in any other known work which Ben Sira might conceivably have used!*

It is true that some of the characteristic features of *Phibis* do not appear in Ben Sira, but these are invariably specifically Egyptian traits, e.g., names of the gods and references to heart and tongue. Several themes highly characteristic of *Phibis* do appear in Ben Sira, however.

---

[149] I am counting Theog. 35–36, 77–78, 81–82, 93–95, 105–8, 115–16, 197–200, 295–99, 323–26, 413–14, 475, 491–94, 497–98, 499–500, 509–10, 575, 643–44, 697–98, 819–20, 929–30 and 1151–52. Cf. above, pp. 29–36.

[150] Above, pp. 55–57.

[151] I am counting *PIns.* i1–24; ii1–18; iii3, 14, 15; iv2–3, 6–7; v20–23; vi1–17; viii4–11, 13, 15–17, 19; ix1–2, 7, 8, 10, 23; x12, 13, 20, 23; xi1, 3, 8, 23; xii18; xiii4–5, 9; xiv3–11; xv13; xvi9; xvii21; xix6–7; xx1; xxiv2; xxv2, 18; xxvi17; xxvii3; xxix16; xxxi19; and xxxii2, 6, 12. Cf. above, pp. 64–96.

The following anecdote underscores to what degree. In an early stage of this study I corresponded about it with a Demoticist who immediately wrote off the possibility of any connection, since, as he put it, had he been Ben Sira, he would have included such striking elements from *Phibis* as the figure of the little bee who produces much, one hundred years as the limit of human life, and the long hymn to creation at the end. Not only, of course, are just these three elements present in Ben Sira, but they were already singled out by Paul Humbert as items of remarkable similarity. My correspondent obviously replied too hastily; yet that very reply is of value here, for it helps the biblical scholar to gain something of the sensitivity of the person who knows the Egyptian literature well and who is able to finger its characteristic traits. Precisely that finger points to Ben Sira.

When I assert that the evidence warrants concluding that Ben Sira used *Phibis* in the same way in which he used Theognis, but to a greater extent, one proviso needs to be attached to that statement, namely, that *Papyrus Insinger* is perhaps not—and certainly not necessarily—the exact form of *Phibis* known to Ben Sira. It appears that, in the Egyptian tradition of wisdom books, each rendering of a work was considered something of an original contribution by the scribe, who normally made certain alterations, deletions, and additions to the work. Each manuscript becomes, then, something of a different text type of the work.[152] François Lexa discussed this aspect of *Phibis* at length and argued from the analogy of the manuscript tradition of *Ptahhotep*, where such apparently "original" reformulations of this famous text can be demonstrated in considerable number.[153] Furthermore, Volten is of the opinion that *Insinger* represents one of two known text types of *Phibis*, and that *Papyrus Carlsberg* V and the Florentine fragments represent the other,[154] so that we now seem to have objective proof of Lexa's assumption. This situation makes possible an explanation both of the striking similarities between *Phibis* and Ben Sira and of the fact that some characteristic aspects of the text of *Phibis* which we have—primarily that of *Papyrus Insinger*—do not appear in Ben Sira—that is, we probably do not possess the exact text type of *Phibis* known to our Jewish sage, although the text type(s) that we do have allow(s) us to see the connection between the two works. Thus, if

---

[152] Cf. again the discussion above, p. 63.

[153] F. Lexa, *Papyrus Insinger. Les enseignements moraux d'un scribe égyptien du premier siècle après J.-C.* (Paris: Paul Geuthner, 1926), 2, §7. Volten has also discussed this phenomenon, especially with regard to *Ani*, in *Studien zum Weisheitsbuch des ANII* (Det kgl. Videnskabernes selskab, Historisk-filologiske Meddelser 13/3; Copenhagen, 1937); and Middendorp, *Stellung*, 98–99, also refers favorably to this work (in support of his theory of alterations in the textual tradition of Ben Sira).

[154] Botti and Volten, "Florentiner-Fragmente," 29. Cf. also Williams, "Sages," 9, who refers to differences in order in the various MSS of *Phibis*.

Lexa, who concurred with the original (late) dating of *Papyrus Insinger*, could write that, "of foreign texts, *Papyrus Insinger* reminds me of the instruction of Jesus, son of Sirach, who was probably under the influence of some sources of *Papyrus Insinger*"[155]—an assertion that is surely justified on the basis of the foregoing analysis—we should be able today to state that, given the revised (earlier) dating of *Papyrus Insinger*, and also the existence of the *Carlsberg Papyri* and of the Florentine fragments of the same work, Ben Sira was under the influence not only of certain *sources* of *Papyrus Insinger* but indeed of an *edition* of the work of which *Papyrus Insinger* is the primary surviving exemplar. Humbert's conclusion, it will be recalled, actually pointed in this direction.[156]

The reader who has been following the argument at all critically may have found himself or herself thinking that some of the alleged cases of influence from *Phibis* upon Ben Sira could well be rather the result of Ben Sira's independent observation and reflection. Why would an upper class Jew have needed an upper class Egyptian to tell him to beat his slave or that he was ruining himself by being an overly protective parent? On principle, I have no objection to this viewpoint and am indeed in sympathy with it. I do *not* wish to engage in parallelomania.[157] But can it be only coincidence that Ben Sira and *Phibis* both place sections of filial piety near the first of their works and statements of *theologia naturae* near the end; *and* that both include in their sections on filial piety the note that the son should not upstage the father; *and* that both lay repeated and substantive emphasis on the need to be cautious and shamefast so as to attain name-immortality; *and* that both use almost the same language in advising staying neither too far away from nor too close to one's lord, including an observable identity of sequence in expression; *and* that both use the example of the productive little bee; *and* that both refer to 100 years as the upper limit of human longevity; *and* that both give catalogues of vices and virtues of women, containing some specifics that are the same; *and* that both advise that coddling a son harms both son and father (in that order); *and* that both agree exactly in the twofold rationale for beating slaves; *and* that both mention the restraining effect of rod and yoke on the unruly passions of slaves; *and* that both use the figure of the rod or the whip as the slave's food? If these similarities are all the coincidental result of independent observation—and I emphasize again that the details are often highly similar—why do these complexes not all appear in any other ancient work?

---

[155] Lexa, *Papyrus Insinger*, 2. 86. Lexa, who was Czech, did not write perfect French, but we understand his meaning. The problem of translating the Demotic text into a second language doubtless in part explains the inadequacies of his translation; cf. W. Spiegelberg, "Beiträge zur Erklärung des Pap. Insinger," *OLZ* 31 (1928) 1025–37.

[156] Cf. above, p. 80.

[157] Cf. again above, p. 1.

The answer, of course, lies in the realization that there are far too many similarities here, including similarities of an idiosyncratic nature, to admit of explanation on the basis of sage observation alone. We are dealing with borrowing. Were it not for the fairly certain dating of *Papyrus Insinger* before the time of Ben Sira, one would have to assume that the borrowing was in the other direction.[158] (If Ben Sira's grandson had his book in Egypt, why could not a pagan have read it?) Because of the time of authorship, however, the lines of transmission must have run from *Phibis* to Ben Sira.

Quite regrettably, external evidence for this theory is lacking, so that readers of this volume who will be convinced only if satisfactory external evidence can be produced will necessarily remain unpersuaded. Could Ben Sira read Demotic? If so, how, when, and where might he have encountered a text of *Phibis*? Naturally one may speculate. An Aramaic translation of *Phibis* existed which someone showed to Ben Sira when he travelled in Egypt. (I am unconvinced by those who take Ben Sira's references to travel as merely rhetorical. He had travelled.) Or a relative in Egypt (why would his grandson have been the first?) sent him a copy. Less likely, a Greek translation of *Phibis* existed, which reached Ben Sira in one of the above ways. Or some Ptolemaic ambassador or business man left such a translation in Jerusalem. As a matter of fact, there is no reason to assume that the man who may well have been the most learned Jew in Jerusalem in his day could not have read Demotic. (There were Gentiles in Jerusalem, too, who may have been more or less learned than our sage.) Why would only modern scholars acquire such skills? There seem to be no examples in Ben Sira of mistranslations of *Phibis*—such would of course carry considerable weight for the argument—and no "Demoticisms." Yet there are also no mistranslations of Theognis and no Grecisms, but numerous students of Ben Sira's work have been convinced that he used Theognis. The skilled translator does not produce mistranslations and does not import the foreign author's style and phraseology into his translation. [On this point, see now the important late note at the end of this chapter, p. 106.] But what about the time involved? If *Phibis* may have been written as late as Ben Sira's own lifetime, could he possibly have read it? Why not? How slow were the mails between Jerusalem and, say, Thebes? Even if there was a long postal strike, surely Ben Sira's remaining lifetime sufficed!

While we see, therefore, that there is no external evidence that Ben Sira used *Phibis*, still there are no objections on external grounds that would render such use impossible or even implausible. We are thus left with the internal evidence just summarized. It seems to me abundant and convincing. I can do no more than rest the case.

---

[158] That was, in fact, the first possibility that I entertained when the extent of these parallels began to be clear to me (cf. "A Hellenistic Egyptian Parallel," 258).

Ben Sira's Manner of Borrowing

If we analyze the ways in which Ben Sira has made use of *Phibis*, as we did with the Theognis and other Egyptian material, we find, not surprisingly, that he has used *Phibis*—with one notable exception—in the same ways in which he has used the other foreign material.

While *Phibis* seems to have been of virtually no help to Ben Sira in expanding the ethical implications of the Torah, it is nevertheless clear that he has understood the section on filial piety[159] to expand the meaning of the fifth commandment; although, we also were able to note, the way in which he builds the section on filial piety is primarily an expansion of Judaic proverbial wisdom.

In addition to that section, one may also list Ben Sira's contrasting discussion of good and bad women[160] and his argument against being an overly protective parent[161] as examples of his use of *Phibis* to expand Judaic proverbial themes, while we should note that the latter may relate at the same time specifically to his ethics of caution. Perhaps we should also include in this category Couroyer's "Egyptianism" about teaching sons. If Ben Sira relied on the content of *Phibis*'s long creation hymn for his own, then that use should also be placed here.

Phibis has also provided, of course, sage observation or advice with which Ben Sira has simply agreed. Here I would list the metaphor of the bee,[162] one hundred years as the limit of human life,[163] the observation that sorrow and care bring illness,[164] and the advice on treatment of slaves.[165]

As we might have expected from *Phibis*'s similar interest in an ethics of caution, Ben Sira has relied, as also in the case of Theognis, quite extensively on *Phibis* in the development of his advice on caution. In addition to the advice against being an overly protective parent (mentioned immediately above), *Phibis*'s advice on caution in friendship[166] and in other associations,[167] his warning against overeating,[168] and his warning against being called different (shameful) things[169] have had their effect on Ben Sira. The Jewish sage has also taken over a portion of

---

[159] Above, pp. 81–82.
[160] Above, pp. 86–87.
[161] Above, p. 88.
[162] Above, p. 71.
[163] Above, p. 71.
[164] Above, pp. 72–74.
[165] Above, pp. 94–96.
[166] Above, pp. 64–65, 82.
[167] Above, pp. 83–84.
[168] Above, pp. 74–75.
[169] Above, p. 82.

the Egyptian sage's caution in opposing the mighty,[170] his caution in associating with the mighty,[171] and his caution in dealing with one's betters (lord, nobles);[172] and he seems to have relied further on *Phibis*'s cautions against being wounded by a slanderer[173] and against squandering,[174] and perhaps on his advice not to trust one's enemy.[175]

Thus we see that Ben Sira has used *Phibis* exactly in the same way in which he used Theognis, although more extensively. Not only has he used *Phibis* material in the same *ways* in which he used Theognis material—and one should include here the fact that Ben Sira never quotes exactly, not even the Bible,[176] although, when he is reformulating a proverb, now and then a word or phrase from his source comes over verbatim, or almost so—he has especially mined *Phibis*, as he also did Theognis, for proverbs that support his ethics of caution. Beyond this, however, I think that it is possible to affirm that Ben Sira has derived *gnomic insight* from *Phibis*, which one could not say about any other foreign texts Ben Sira is known to have used. He appears in fact to have absorbed the cautious, shamefast, name-protective ethics which he has encountered in *Phibis* and—as far as we can tell—nowhere else. We see this especially clearly when Ben Sira seems to rely on *Phibis* for a statement on the importance of one's enduring name,[177] or when both works attest the prevalence of a shame-based ethics of caution.[178] Surely Ben Sira has relied on *Phibis* far more heavily than on any other foreign literature; and the Egyptian work has indeed provided to him his basic ethical position. When Ben Sira, therefore, summarizes his position at the conclusion of the body of his work (41:13) with the simple proverb,

> *ṭwbt ḥy ymy mspr   wṭwbt šm ymy 'yn mspr,*
> *The value of a* life lasts for *a number of* days,
> But the *value* of a name for days without number,

he has altered traditional Judaic eudaemonism in the direction of traditional Egyptian eudaemonism, where the immortality of the name was a prominent part of the standard and ancient hope. The *way* in which this position is expressed in Ben Sira and *Phibis*, as well as other similarities of detail, lead us to the conclusion that it was the work of *Phibis* that opened Ben Sira's eyes to this position, which he considered superior to

---

170 Above, p. 83.
171 Above, p. 84.
172 Above, pp. 85, 92–93.
173 Above, p. 85.
174 Above, pp. 85–86.
175 Above, p. 85.
176 Peters, *Jesus Sirach*, XLVII: "He indeed quotes verbatim relatively seldom."
177 Above, pp. 84–85.
178 Above, pp. 93–94.

(for reasons at which we might only guess) but not disharmonious with his own Judaic traditions.

Possible Relation to Other Demotic Works

We can perhaps bring the relation between *Phibis* and Ben Sira, finally, into still clearer focus if we give some attention to other Demotic gnomic works which Ben Sira might conceivably have known, especially *The Instructions of 'Onchsheshonqy*, a work which was not known to Paul Humbert.[179] This work circulated in the time of *Phibis*, as can be seen in the similarities in the Demotic scripts of the papyri of *'Onchsheshonqy* and of *Papyrus Insinger*;[180] internal evidence, however, shows that its origin must lie in the late pre-Ptolemaic period.[181] Like *Phibis*, Ben Sira, or the Book of Proverbs, *'Onchsheshonqy* is a collection of gnomic maxims and advice, yet already here one of the major differences between *'Onchsheshonqy* on the one hand and Ben Sira and *Phibis* on the other is to be observed, for *'Onchsheshonqy* provides only a random collection of proverbs and reveals none of the organization that marks *Phibis* and Ben Sira.

There are some similarities, to be sure. Thus *'Onch.* vii18 observes that "a servant who is not beaten is full of scorn," which is reminiscent of Sir 33:25–27 (above, pp. 95–96), but the similarity is not as close as that between Sir 33:24 and *PIns.* xiv8.[182] One may also note *'Onch.* vii23–24: "Do not speak hastily lest you give offense. Do not say the first thing that comes into your head," with which one might compare Sir 20:18–19:

> A slip on the pavement is better than a (slip) of the tongue;
>> So doth the fall of the wicked come swiftly.
> *An ungracious person [is like] an untimely story;*
>> *In the mouth of the untrained it perseveres.*

Middendorp, however, cites a similar saying of Zeno: "It is better to slip with the feet than with the tongue."[183] Thus Middendorp repeats the judgment of Smend that we likely have to do with a general Semitic saying here.[184] The saying of Zeno is in any case an exact parallel to Ben Sira; *'Onchsheshonqy*'s advice is only generally similar.

---

[179] *'Onchsheshonqy* was first published by S. R. K. Glanville in *Catalogue of Demotic Papyri in the British Museum, 2: The Instructions of 'Onshsheshonqy (British Museum Papyrus 10508), Part I: Introduction, transliteration, translation, notes, and plates* (London: Trustees of the British Museum, 1955).

[180] Ibid., xii.

[181] Ibid. Glanville referred especially to the pharaonic elements.

[182] Above, p. 95.

[183] Text in *Diogenes Laertii, Vitae philosophorum, 2* (Oxford: Clarendon Press, 1964) 7.26; my translation.

[184] Middendorp, *Stellung*, 20.

'Onch. viii8 states the obvious truth that "there is no man who does not die," and this is certainly similar to Sir 41:3–4a:

> Fear not Death, (it is) thy destiny,
>> Remember that the former and the latter (share it) with thee.
> This is the portion of all flesh from God,
>> And how canst thou *reject* the *law* of the Most High!

One may also recall, however, the likely reliance of Ben Sira on biblical themes at this point.[185]

'Onch. xi21–22, "Do not say 'The sinner (?) against God lives to-day,' but look to the end. Say (rather) 'A fortunate fate is at the end of old age,'" might bring to mind Sir 11:28: "Before death *do not* pronounce *a* man happy; For by his latter end a man shall be known"; yet the famous saying of Solon is almost certainly quoted here.[186] Or one might be reminded of Sir 41:10–12:

> All that is of naught returneth to naught,
>> So the *profane* man,—from nothingness to nothingness.
> A *vapor* is man (concerning) his body,
>> But the name of the pious shall not be cut off.
> Be in fear for thy name, for that abideth longer for thee
>> Than thousands of treasures *of wisdom.*

Yet, Ben Sira begins this passage with an unmistakable reference to Qoheleth (ephemerality of existence, *hbl*—used only one other time in Ben Sira!), whose position he then modifies to refer only to the body, after which he states his own opinion—as, of course, superior.[187] *PIns.* xx1 is closer, as we saw above,[188] to Ben Sira's own position than is 'Onch. xi21–22.

In 'Onch. xiv8 one reads, "When you make a companion of (even) a wise man whose mind you do not know, do not open your mind to him," which bears some resemblance to Ben Sira's statement of caution in friendship in 6:7; but, again, both *PIns.* xi23; xii18 and Xenophon offer closer parallels.[189] So also when 'Onchsheshonqy once (xvii26) mentions shame as a protection for one's name: "Be modest, that your reputation may increase in the hearts of all men." Here one may only recall *Phibis's* and Ben Sira's extensive treatments of this theme.[190]

When 'Onchsheshonqy writes in xxi22, "Better death than want,"

---

[185] Above, pp. 35–36.

[186] Cf. Middendorp, *Stellung*, 17.

[187] In other words, Ben Sira quotes Qoheleth in order to modify Qoheleth's position in the direction of his own. On this technique, cf. Gordis, "Quotations," esp. pp. 229–34.

[188] Above, pp. 84–85.

[189] Above, pp. 82, 44, 64–65.

[190] Above, pp. 93–94.

one will be reminded, of course, of Sir 30:17, "Better death than an *empty* life, And eternal rest than continual pain"; but Qoheleth also expressed the thought.[191]

Finally, one may note that 'Onchsheshonqy, in col. xxv, contains a series of statements on female vices and virtues; yet none of the statements here has an exact equivalent in Ben Sira, and the catalogues of female vices and virtues in Ben Sira and *Phibis* remain noticeably close.[192]

The situation is similar with *Papyrus Louvre* 2414.[193] *PLouvre* 2414ii2, "Do not make a comrade of an evil man," may remind one of Sir 8:15; but one would also have to note the similarity between the latter and Prov 22:24.

One proverb from this papyrus is indeed close to Ben Sira—*PLouvre* 2414iii11–12: "Do not walk with a foolish man. Do not stay to hear his speech." Thus Sir 8:17: "Take no counsel with a fool, For he will not be able to keep thy *counsel*." That is, however, the extent of close parallels between Ben Sira and *Papyrus Louvre* 2414.

One may therefore see that, while there are some possible connections (parallels, in any case) between Ben Sira and other Demotic wisdom papyri that are more or less contemporary with Ben Sira and with *Phibis* and that are somewhat similar to them in style and in advice, still the fact remains that *Phibis* is much more like Ben Sira than such other literature, and that *Phibis* is *more* like Ben Sira, in both style and content, than is *any other collection of proverbs, Theognis included, save only the Book of Proverbs itself.* The likely explanation of this fact is that Ben Sira has read *Phibis*, has been much impressed by it, and has taken over not only individual proverbs from it, but much of its format as well and, indeed, its basic orientation toward life—namely, that one must be cautious and shamefast in order to secure for oneself an everlasting good name.

The originality that one may attribute to Ben Sira lies more in his choice and manner of appropriation of accumulated wisdom than in novel thoughts. In this way, of course, a tradition grows and moves but remains an identifiable tradition. Ben Sira relied on his Judaic tradition—both on the wisdom tradition and on the (Deuteronomic)

191 Above, p. 34.

192 Above, pp. 86–87.

193 Cf. Volten, "Die moralischen Lehren des demotischen Pap. Louvre 2414," *Studi in memoria di Ippolito Rosellini* (ed. A. Ev. Breccia; Pisa: Lischi, 1955), 2. 269–80+Taf. XXXIV, XXXV. Regarding this papyrus, Volten notes that "in some cases, the source appears to have been the great Demotic Wisdom Book [i.e., *Phibis*]. . . . It is naturally also possible and perhaps more probable that the author of [*PLouvre* 2414] and the author of [*Phibis*] both used older wisdom literature," ibid., 280.

tradition of Torah; but he also used and Judaized Hellenic sources, and he used and Judaized Egyptian sources to an even greater extent. In the matter of the name-shame-caution ethics that so characterises both Ben Sira and *Phibis,* Ben Sira seems actually to have derived gnomic insight from the Egyptian work. He emphasized the research aspect of his work, and our analysis has confirmed that he was not merely painting an ideal portrait when he did so.

There was nothing remarkable or forbidden to Ben Sira in reading and using foreign literature. Wisdom belonged to all people; it was acquisitive and international—which is our modern way of saying what Ben Sira said in 39:1-4, that the sage was one "Who searcheth out the wisdom of all the ancients, And is occupied with the prophets; . . . Who travelleth through the lands of other peoples, Testeth good and evil among men." The particular revelation to Israel did not deny the existence of wisdom elsewhere, and Ben Sira wanted it all. Although the Most High had said to Wisdom, "Let thy dwelling-place be in Jacob, And in Israel take up thine inheritance" (Sir 24:8), nevertheless originally (v 6) "Over the waves of the sea, and over all the earth, And over every people and nation [Wisdom] held sway."

o o o

LATE NOTE: After this work had already been set in final page proofs, evidence came to light of Jewish use of both Aramaic and Demotic in a bilingual setting in Ben Sira's day. It was reported in the *New York Times* of 11 October 1982, Section II, p. 1, that Professor Richard C. Steiner of the Bernard Revel Graduate School of Yeshiva University had determined that a manuscript in Demotic script, long undeciphered and thought to be mere gibberish, is in reality portions of Psalm 20 (and perhaps other things, in addition) in Aramaic, but written in Demotic Script—that is, Aramaic transliterated into Demotic. I take this to be something like the ancient equivalent of the current practice in this country of printing transliterations of Hebrew in Roman letters in prayer books for synagogue use. The manuscript, now the property of the Pierpont Morgan Library, was discovered in Thebes in the nineteenth century, and Professor Steiner thus takes it perhaps to have originated in the Jewish community at Edfu, up river from Thebes. The script is that of the second century B.C.E. If, therefore, Jews in upper Egypt in Ben Sira's day were bilingual with Aramaic and Demotic, then the linguistic context that would have allowed Ben Sira to become acquainted with the content of *Phibis* is absolutely attested.

Professor Steiner plans to present a full treatment of the issue, in cooperation with Professor Charles F. Nims, in a forthcoming issue of *JAOS.* I am grateful to Professor H.-M. Schenke of the Humboldt University in Berlin for directing my attention to the *New York Times* article.

SELECTED BIBLIOGRAPHY

TEXTS AND TRANSLATIONS

(Aeschylus) *Eschyle 2: Agamemnon—Les choéphores—Les euménides*. Paris: Societé d'édition "Les Belles Lettres," 1925.

ANET. 3d ed. with supplement. Princeton: Princeton University Press, 1969.

(Ben Sira) Vattioni, Francesco, ed. *Ecclesiastico. Testo Ebraico con apparato critico e versioni greca, latina e siriaca*. Testi 1. Naples: Istituto Orientale di Napoli, 1968.

(Ben Sira) Ziegler, Joseph, ed. *Sapientia Iesu Filii Sirach*. Septuaginta: Vetus Testamentum Graecum 12/2. Göttingen: Vandenhoeck & Ruprecht, 1965.

Diogenes Laertii, Vitae philosophorum 2. Oxford: Clarendon Press, 1964.

Erman, Adolf. *The Ancient Egyptians. A Sourcebook of Their Writings*. New York: Harper & Row, 1966.

(Euripides) *Bacchae of Euripides, The*. Cambridge: Cambridge University Press, 1900.

Euripides, Medea. Oxford: Oxford University Press, 1969.

Hesiod, the Homeric Hymns, and Homerica. LCL. Cambridge, Mass.: Harvard University Press, 1967.

Homeri Ilias. Leipzig: Teubner, 1888.

Homer's Odyssey. 2 vols. 2d ed. Oxford: Clarendon Press, 1886.

(Homer) *Iliad of Homer, The*. Translated by Richmond Lattimore. Chicago and London: University of Chicago Press, 1951.

(Homer) *Odyssey of Homer, The*. Translated by Richmond Lattimore. New York, et al.: Harper & Row, 1967.

Josephus 1. LCL. New York: Putnam's, 1926.

('Onchsheshonqy) *Catalogue of Demotic Papyri in the British Museum 2: The Instructions of 'Onchsheshonqy (British Museum Papyrus 10508)* Part 1: Introduction, transliteration, translation, notes, and plates, ed. S. R. K. Glanville. London: Trustees of the British Museum, 1955.

(*Phibis*) Bissing, Fr. W. Freiherr von, ed. and trans. *Altägyptische Lebensweisheit*. Zurich: Artemis, 1955.

(*Phibis*) Botti, Giuseppi, and Volten, Aksel. "Florentiner-Fragmente zum Texte des *Pap. Insinger*." *AcOr* 25 (1960) 29–42.

(*Phibis*) Lexa, François. *Papyrus Insinger. Les enseignements moraux d'un scribe égyptien du premier siècle après J.-C.* 2 vols. Paris: Geuthner, 1926.

(*Phibis*) *Monuments égyptiens du musée d'antiquités des pays-bas à Leide.* 34e livraison: *Suten-χeft, le livre royal. Papyrus Démotique Insinger.* Transcription, with introduction by W. Pleyte and P. A. A. Boeser. Leiden: Brill, 1899. Supplement: Edition en phototypie, 1905.

Philonis Alexandrini, Opera Quae Supersunt, ed. Leopoldus Cohn, Paulus Wendland, Sigofredus Reiter. 6 vols. Editio minor. Berlin: Georg Reimer, 1896–1915.

Platonis Opera 5. Oxford: Clarendon Press, 1913.

(*PLouvre* 2414) Volten, Aksel. "Die moralischen Lehren des demotischen Pap. Louvre 2414." *Studi in memoria di Ippolito Rosellini.* 269–80 +Tafeln XXXIV–XXXV. Edited by A. Ev. Breccia. Pisa: Lischi, 1955.

(Theognis) *Elegy and Iambus with the Anacreontea* 1. LCL. Cambridge, Mass.: Harvard University Press, 1968.

Xenophon. *Memorabilia and Oeconomicus.* LCL. New York: Putnam's, 1923.

STANDARD REFERENCE WORKS

Barthélemy, D., and Rickenbacher, O. *Konkordanz zum hebräischen Sirach.* Göttingen: Vandenhoeck & Ruprecht, 1973.

Oxford Classical Dictionary, The. 2d ed. Oxford: Clarendon Press, 1970.

COMMENTARIES

Box, G. H., and Oesterley, W. O. E. "The Book of Sirach." *APOT* 1. 268–517.

Dibelius, Martin. *An die Kolosser, Epheser, an Philemon.* 3d ed. Edited by Heinrich Greeven. HNT 12. Tübingen: Mohr (Siebeck), 1953.

Duesberg, Hilaire, and Auvray, Paul, ed. *Le livre de l'Ecclésiastique.* La Sainte Bible. Paris: Editions du Cerf, 1958.

Edersheim, A. "Ecclesiasticus." *The Holy Bible . . . with an Explanatory and Critical Commentary: Apocrypha* 2. 1–239. Edited by Henry Wace. London: John Murray, 1888.

Fritzsche, Otto Fridolin. *Kurzgefasstes exegetisches Handbuch zu den Apokryphen des Alten Testamentes.* Fünfte Lieferung: *Die Weisheit Jesus-Sirach's.* Leipzig: S. Hirzel, 1859.

Gordis, Robert. *The Book of God and Man. A Study of Job.* Chicago and London: University of Chicago Press, 1965.

————. *Koheleth—the Man and His World. A Study of Ecclesiastes.* 3d ed. New York: Schocken, 1968.

————. *The Song of Songs and Lamentations. A Study, Modern*

Translation and Commentary. New York: KTAV, 1974.

Kroeber, Rudi. *Der Prediger. Hebräisch und deutsch.* Schriften und Quellen der alten Welt 13. Berlin: Akademie-Verlag, 1963.

Lévi, Israel. *L'Ecclésiastique ou la Sagesse de Jésus, fils de Sira.* 2 parts. Paris: Ernest Leroux, 1898-1901.

Peters, Norbert. *Das Buch Jesus Sirach oder Ecclesiasticus.* EHAT 25. Münster in Westf.: Aschendorff, 1913.

Ryssel, Victor. "Die Sprüche Jesus', des Sohnes Sirachs." *Die Apokryphen und Pseudepigraphen des Alten Testaments* 1: *Die Apokryphen des Alten Testaments,* 230-475. Edited by E. Kautzsch. Tübingen: Mohr (Siebeck), 1900.

Sgl, Mšh Ṣby. *Spr Bn Syr' Hšlm.* Yrwšlym: Mwsd By'lyq, 1958. (Hebrew).

Smend, Rudolf. *Die Weisheit des Jesus Sirach.* Berlin: Georg Reimer, 1906.

Spicq, C. "L'Ecclésiastique." *La Sainte Bible,* 529-841. Edited by Louis Pirot and Albert Clamer. Paris: Letouzey et Ané, 1951.

Toy, Crawford H. *A Critical and Exegetical Commentary on The Book of Proverbs.* ICC. New York: Scribner's, 1908.

Van der Horst, P. W. *The Sentences of Pseudo-Phocylides.* SVTP. Leiden: Brill, 1978.

Volz, Paul. *Hiob und Weisheit.* Die Schriften des Alten Testaments 3/2. 2d ed. Göttingen: Vandenhoeck & Ruprecht, 1921.

OTHER LITERATURE

Bauckmann, Ernst Günter. "Die Proverbien und die Sprüche des Jesus Sirach." *ZAW* 72 (1960) 33-63.

Bigot, L. "Livre de l'Ecclésiastique." *DTC* 4/2 (1920), cols. 2025-54.

Bolkestein, Hendrik. *Wohltätigkeit und Armenpflege im vorchristlichen Altertum.* Groningen: Bouma, 1967.

Burkill, T. A. "Ecclesiasticus." *IDB* 2 (1962) 13-21.

Conzelmann, Hans. "The Mother of Wisdom." *The Future of Our Religious Past,* 230-43. Edited by James M. Robinson. New York, *et al.*: Harper & Row, 1971.

Couard, L. *Die religiösen und sittlichen Anschauungen der alttestamentlichen Apokryphen und Pseudepigraphen.* Gütersloh: Bertelsmann, 1909.

Couroyer, B. "Un égyptianisme dans Ben Sira IV, 11." *RB* 82 (1975) 206-17.

Crenshaw, James L. *Old Testament Wisdom. An Introduction.* Atlanta: John Knox, 1981.

————. "The Problem of Theodicy in Sirach: On Human Bondage." *JBL* 94 (1975) 47-64.

————. *Prophetic Conflict. Its Effect Upon Israelite Religion.* BZAW

124. Berlin and New York: de Gruyter, 1971.

———, ed. *Studies in Ancient Israelite Wisdom*. New York: KTAV, 1976.

Fuss, Werner. "Tradition und Komposition in Buche Jesus Sirach." Dissertation Tübingen, 1962.

Gemser, B. "The Instructions of '*Onchsheshonqy* and Biblical Wisdom Literature." *Studies in Ancient Israelite Wisdom*, 134–60. (See Crenshaw.)

Gilbert, M. "L'éloge de la Sagesse (*Siracide* 24)." *RTL* 5 (1974) 326–48.

Glasson, T. Fr. *Greek Influence in Jewish Eschatology*. London: S. P. C. K., 1961.

Gordis, Robert. "Quotations in Wisdom Literature." *Studies in Ancient Israelite Wisdom*, 220–44. (See Crenshaw.)

———. "The Social Background of Wisdom Literature." *HUCA* 18 (1944) 77–118.

Hadas, Moses. *Hellenistic Culture, Fusion and Diffusion*. New York: Columbia University Press, 1959.

Hadot, Jean. *Penchant mauvais et volonté libre dans la Sagesse de Ben Sira*. Brussels: Presses Universitaires, 1970.

Haspecker, Josef. *Gottesfurcht bei Jesus Sirach*. AnBib 30. Rome: Pontificio Instituto Biblico, 1967.

Hengel, Martin. *Judaism and Hellenism*. 2 vols. Philadelphia: Fortress, 1974.

Hermisson, H.-J. *Studien zur israelitischen Spruch-Weisheit*. WMANT 28. Neukirchen-Vluyn: Neukirchener Verlag, 1968.

Humbert, Paul. *Recherches sur les sources égyptiennes de la littérature sapientiale d'Israël*. Mémoires de l'Université de Neuchatel 7. Neuchatel: Secrétariat de l'Université, 1929.

Hughes, H. Maldwyn. *The Ethics of Jewish Aprocryphal Literature*. London: Robert Culley, n. d. [1910].

Kaiser, Otto. "Die Begründung der Sittlichkeit im Buche Jesus Sirach." *ZTK* 55 (1958) 51–63.

Lang, Bernhard. *Frau Weisheit: Deutung einer biblischen Gestalt*. Düsseldorf: Patmos, 1975.

———. "Schule und Unterricht im alten Israel." *La Sagesse de l'Ancien Testament*, 186–201. Edited by M. Gilbert. BETL 51. Gembloux: Duculot, 1979.

McKane, William. *Prophets and Wise Men*. SBT 44. Naperville, Ill.: Allenson, 1965.

———. *Proverbs. A New Approach*. Old Testament Library. Philadelphia: Westminster, 1970.

Marböck, Johannes. Review of Middendorp, Theophil, *Die Stellung Jesu Ben Siras zwischen Judentum und Hellenismus*. VT 24 (1974) 510–13.

_____. *Weisheit im Wandel. Untersuchungen zur Weisheitstheologie bei Ben Sira*. BBB 37. Bonn: Peter Hanstein, 1971.

Michaelis, Dieter. "Das Buch Jesus Sirach als typischer Ausdruck für das Gottesverhältnis des nachalttestamentlichen Menschen." *TLZ* 83 (1958) 601–8.

Middendorp, Theophil. *Die Stellung Jesu Ben Siras zwischen Judentum und Hellenismus*. Leiden: Brill, 1973.

Moore, George Foot. *Judaism in the First Centuries of the Christian Era*. 2 vols. New York: Schocken, 1971.

Morenz, Siegfried. "Eine weitere Spur der Weisheit Amenopes in der Bibel." *Zeitschrift für ägyptische Sprache und Altertumskunde* 84 (1959) 79–80.

Murphy, Roland E. "Hebrew Wisdom." *JAOS* 101 (1981) 21–34.

Pautrel, Raymond. "Ben Sira et le stöicisme." *RSR* 51 (1963) 535–49.

Pfeiffer, Robert H. *History of New Testament Times With an Introduction to the Aprocrypha*. New York: Harper & Brothers, 1949.

Pohlenz, Max. *Die Stoa*. 3d ed. Göttingen: Vandenhoeck & Ruprecht, 1964.

Rad, Gerhard von. *Old Testament Theology*. 2 vols. New York and Evanston: Harper & Row, 1962.

_____. *Wisdom in Israel*. Nashville and New York: Abingdon, 1972.

Rankin, O. S. *Israel's Wisdom Literature*. Edinburgh: T. & T. Clark, n. d. [1936].

Rickenbacher, Otto. *Weisheitsperikopen bei Ben Sira*. Orbis biblicus et orientalis 1. Freiburg/Schweiz: Universitätsverlag, 1973.

Ringgren, Helmer. *Word and Wisdom*. Lund: Håkan Ohlssons Boktryckeri, 1947.

Rose, H. J. *A Handbook of Greek Literature from Homer to the Age of Lucian*. New York: Dutton, 1960.

Rylaarsdam, J. Coert. *Revelation in Jewish Wisdom Literature*. Chicago: University of Chicago Press, 1946.

Sanders, E. P. *Paul and Palestinian Judaism. A Comparison of Patterns of Religion*. Philadelphia: Fortress, 1977.

Sanders, Jack T. "A Hellenistic Egyptian Parallel to Ben Sira." *JBL* 97 (1978) 257–58.

_____. "Ben Sira's Ethics of Caution." *HUCA* 50 (1979) 73–106.

Sandmel, Samuel. "Parallelomania." *JBL* 81 (1962) 1–13.

Siebeneck, Robert T. "May Their Bones Return to Life!—Sirach's Praise of the Fathers." *CBQ* 21 (1959) 411–28.

Skehan, Patrick W. "Structures in Poems on Wisdom: Proverbs 8 and Sirach 24." *CBQ* 41 (1979) 365–79.

_____. *Studies in Israelite Poetry and Wisdom*. CBQMS 1. Washington: Catholic Biblical Association of America, 1971.

Spiegelberg, Wilhelm. "Beiträge zur Erklärung des *Pap. Insinger.*" *OLZ* 31 (1928) 1025–37.

Treves, M. *Studi su Gesù ben Sirach.* Estratto da la Rassegna Mensile di Israel 22/9–10. Città di castello, 1956.

Vawter, Bruce. "Prov. 22: Wisdom and Creation." *JBL* 99 (1980) 205–16.

Volten, Aksel. *Das demotische Weisheitsbuch.* Copenhagen: Munksgaard, 1941.

―――. *Studien zum Weisheitsbuch des ANII.* Det kgl. Videnskabernes selskab, Historisk-filologiske Meddelser 13/3. Copenhagen, 1937.

Whitley, Charles F. *Koheleth. His Language and Thought.* BZAW 148. Berlin and New York: de Gruyter, 1979.

Wilckens, Ulrich. "*sophia, ktl.*" *TDNT* 7 (1971) 465–528.

Williams, R. J. "The Sages of Ancient Egypt in the Light of Recent Scholarship." *JAOS* 101 (1981) 1–19.

Winston, David. "Freedom and Determinism in Greek Philosophy and Jewish Hellenistic Wisdom." *Studia Philonica* 2 (1973) 40–50.

Würthwein, Ernst. "Egyptian Wisdom and the Old Testament." *Studies in Ancient Israelite Wisdom,* 113–33. (See Crenshaw.)

Ziener, Georg. *Die theologische Begriffssprache im Buche der Weisheit.* BBB 11. Bonn: Peter Hanstein, 1956.

INDEXES

I. Bible (Including Apocrypha)

II. Other Ancient Literature and Authors

III. Modern Authors

LaVergne, TN USA
07 October 2010

200012LV00002B/7/A